Remade for Happiness

FULTON J. SHEEN

Remade for Happiness

IGNATIUS PRESS   SAN FRANCISCO

First edition: *Preface to Religion*
© 1946 by P. J. Kenedy & Sons, New York

Nihil Obstat: John M. A. Fearns, S.T.D.
                    Censor Librorum
Imprimatur: + Francis Cardinal Spellman
                    Archbishop of New York
                    April 4, 1946

Cover illustration:
The caterpillar and butterfly illustration originally
appeared as a plate in *Europas bekannteste Schmetterlinge*
1895, F. Nemos, Oestergaard Verlag, Berlin

Cover design by Milo Persic

Published in 2014 by Ignatius Press, San Francisco
with permission of P. J. Kenedy & Sons, Berkeley Heights, N.J.
Foreword by Jennifer Fulwiler © 2014 by Ignatius Press
All rights reserved
ISBN 978-1-58617-783-6
Library of Congress Control Number 2014905850
Printed in the United States of America ∞

CONTENTS

FOREWORD

by
Jennifer Fulwiler

The DuMont Television Network needed to fill a hole in their schedule, an 8:00 P.M. slot that was up against television titans on other networks. There was no hope for any show in such a position; industry jargon called it a "graveyard slot". In a spirit of public service, DuMont offered a rotating selection of religious programming, featuring a rabbi, a Protestant pastor, and a Catholic bishop named Fulton Sheen.

Two of the shows never gained traction and eventually faded away. But something strange happened with the other one.

Life Is Worth Living, Bishop Sheen's show, caught people's notice. Instantly, it had an audience—and the audience would soon explode in size, growing exponentially in the months and years that followed. Despite the late hour, the seemingly unexciting subject matter, and the big budgets and glitzy productions of the competing shows, viewers all across America began to schedule their evenings around the Bishop who spoke about faith while drawing on a chalkboard.

Within two months, the number of stations that carried the show rose from three to fifteen. Just four years later, *Life Is Worth Living* had a massive audience, with millions of people tuning in to each episode. Overstuffed mailbags brought in almost ten thousand viewer letters each week. Bishop Sheen won an Emmy Award for "Most Outstanding Television Personality". His show had never been expected to be popular at all—let alone be a source of competition for mega-celebrities like Milton Berle and Frank Sinatra—yet Sheen soared past Sinatra in the ratings, and eventually he topped Berle.

The utterly unexpected and meteoric rise of Bishop Fulton Sheen is one of the most remarkable stories in the history of television. Media analysts attribute his shocking success to his unparalleled skills as an orator. Religious observers give credit to the grace of God. Certainly both Sheen's talent and divine intervention were factors, yet there is another, often-overlooked explanation for why an entire nation tuned in to the humble show of a Catholic bishop:

Sheen knew the secret to happiness.

Venerable Archbishop Sheen lived at the dawn of the cultural revolution that would reach its apex in the 1960s and 1970s, and he was one of the first to spot it. He felt the first tremors of the social upheaval that would eventually rock the entire Western world.

Presciently, he understood that not only would abandoning Judeo-Christian values put people's souls in danger, but it would make them miserable.

Remade for Happiness, originally published in 1946 as *Preface to Religion*, is Sheen's warning flare to a people adrift. With powerful, plainspoken prose, he systematically explains that a culture seeking satisfaction in worldly amusements will be a culture of restlessness and misery. Sheen begins with the archetypal moment of a child receiving a lavish spread of Christmas presents, only to realize he's still not completely happy. From there he takes the reader through a step-by-step analysis of why true fulfillment can only be found in God, through his Church. Each short chapter is packed with jaw-dropping insights worthy of a weighty philosophical tome, yet has the friendly, accessible style of a conversation over a cup of coffee with a kindly parish priest.

Sheen was a man of his time, and the modern reader smiles at references to a bygone culture where men tipped their hats at ladies and children might give their fathers penny cigars as gifts. Yet the reader also senses that Sheen is aware of the fleetingness of his own era, that the venerable Archbishop would have been the first to predict that the social constructs he references would seem antiquated little more than a half-century later. In Chapter 14 he writes, "Your knowledge will get out of date; your statistics will be old next month; the theories you learned in college are already antiquated. But love never gets out of date."

Sheen's insights are timeless. The wisdom that he originally laid out in this book is the same wisdom that led his simple television show to be a smash hit a decade later, and that makes *Remade for Happiness* an essential read for anyone living in twenty-first century, post-Christian culture. It is not a wisdom confined to a certain time and place on earth, because it is not of this earth at all.

Perhaps Milton Berle said it best. When asked about the millions of viewers Sheen drew away from his own, competing show, Berle quipped, "He's got better writers—Matthew, Mark, Luke, and John!"

By going back to the very basic truths about the human experience—who we are, who God is, how we can find fulfillment—Sheen essentially offers an owner's manual to the human soul. It is not a manual created by him, but rather an articulation of the one revealed by God through His Word and His Church. Such a book is desperately needed in our age, an age when there could hardly be more confusion about what it means to be human, and to be happy. As much as his message resonated with the people of his own time, we need his cogent, concise explanation of the real secret to happiness now more than ever.

CHAPTER ONE

Are You Happy?

If you saw hordes of peoples tramping the fields, with axes in their hands and pans strapped to their shoulders, you would conclude that those people had not found all the gold they wanted. If you saw armies of nurses and doctors riding ambulances or carrying cots, you would conclude that health had not been found. When you see people crowding into theaters, charging cocktail bars, seeking new thrills in a spirit of restlessness, you would conclude that they have not yet found pleasure, otherwise they would not be looking for it.

The very fact that you can conceive of greater happiness than you possess now is a proof that you are not happy. If you were perfect, you would be happy. There is no doubt that at one time or another in your life you attained that which you believed would make you happy, but when you got what you wanted were you happy?

Do you remember when you were a child, how ardently you looked forward to Christmas? How happy you thought you would be, with your fill of cakes, your hands glutted with toys, and your eyes dancing with the lights on the tree!

Christmas came, and after you had eaten your fill, blown out the last Christmas light, and played till your toys no longer amused, you climbed into your bed, and said in your own little heart of hearts, that somehow or other it did not quite come up to your expectations. Have you not lived that experience over a thousand times since?

You looked forward to the joys of travel, but when weary feet carried you home, you admitted that the two happiest days were the day you left home and the day you got back. Perhaps it was marriage that you thought would bring you perfect happiness. Even though it did bring a measure of happiness, you admit that you now take your companion's love for granted.

Why is it that all love songs are about "how happy we *will be*"; who ever hears a song about "how happy we are"? The beloved may be the sun of all delight, but sooner or later someone becomes disillusioned

> *Observing how*
> *He had assigned to his dear mistress more*
> *Than it is proper to concede to mortals.*
> —Lucretius

One is never thirsty at the border of the well.

Perhaps it was wealth you wanted. You got it, and now you are afraid of losing it. "A golden bit does not make the better horse." A man's happiness truly does not consist in the abundance of the things he possesses. Maybe it was a desire to be well-known that you craved. You did become well-known only to find that reputation is like a ball: as soon as it starts rolling, men begin to kick it around.

The fact is: you want to be perfectly happy, but you are not. Your life has been a series of disappointments, shocks, and disillusionments. How have you reacted to your disappointments? Either you became cynical or else you became religious.

If you became cynical, you decided that, since life is a snare and a delusion, you ought to get as much fun out of it as possible. In such a case you clutched at every titillation and excitement your senses afforded, making your life an incessant quest of what you called a "good time". Or else you reacted to disappointments by becoming religious and saying: "If I want happiness, I must have been made for it. If I am disappointed here, it must be that I am seeking happiness in the wrong places. I must look for it somewhere else, namely, in God."

Here is a fallacy to the first reaction: believing that the purpose of life is to get as much pleasure out of it as possible. This would be the right attitude if you were just an animal. But you have a soul as well as a body. Hence, there are joys in life as well as pleasures.

There is a world of difference between the two. Pleasure is of the body; joy is of the mind and heart. Lobster Newburg gives pleasure to certain people, but not even the most avid lobster fans would ever say that it made them joyful. You can quickly become tired of pleasures, but you never tire of joys. A boy thinks he never could get too much ice cream, but he soon discovers there is just not enough boy.

A pleasure can be increased to a point where it ceases to be a pleasure; it may even begin to be a pain if carried beyond a certain point; for example, tickling or drinking. But the joy of a good conscience, or the joy of a First Communion, or the discovery of a truth, never turns to pain.

Man can become dizzy from the pleasure of drink, but no man ever became dizzy from the joy of prayer. A light can be so bright it will blind the eye, but no idea was ever so bright as to kill the mind; in fact, the stronger and clearer the idea, the greater its joy. If, therefore, you live for pleasure, you are missing the joys of life.

Furthermore, have you noticed that as your desire for pleasure increased, the satisfaction from the pleasure decreased? The dope fiend, to have an equal pleasure, must increase his dose. Do you think a philosophy of life is right that is based on the law of diminishing returns? If you were made for pleasure, why should your capacity for pleasure diminish with the years instead of increasing?

Then, too, have you observed that your pleasures were always greater in anticipation than in realization? With the joys of the spirit, it is just the contrary. The cross, for example, is unattractive in prospect, but is sweet in possession. To Judas, the prospect of thirty pieces of silver was attractive, but he brought back his thirty pieces of silver. He got what he wanted and it filled him with disgust.

If your philosophy is always to have a good time, you have long ago discovered that you never really have a good time, for you are always in pursuit of happiness without ever capturing it. By a twist of nature, you make your happiness consist in the quest for happiness, rather than in happiness itself, just as so many modern professors much prefer to seek the truth than to find it. You thus become most hungry where you are most satisfied.

When the first thrill of ownership is gone, and your possessions begin to cloy, your sole happiness now is in pursuit of more possessions. You turn the pages of life, but you never read the book.

That is why those who live only for pleasure become cynical in middle age. A cynic has been defined as one who knows the price of everything and the value of nothing. You blame things, rather than self. If you are married, you say: "If I had another husband, or another wife, I could be happy." Or you say, "If I had another job ...", or, "If I visited another night-club ...", or, "If I were in another city, I would be happy." In every instance, you make happiness *extrinsic* to yourself. No wonder *you* are never happy. You are chasing mirages until death overtakes you.

Never will you find the happiness you crave because your desires conflict. Despite the advertisements "Eat and dance", you cannot do both at the same time. There is an exclusiveness about certain pleasures; they cannot be enjoyed in company with others. You cannot enjoy a good book and a football game at the same time. You cannot make a club sandwich of the pleasures of swimming and skiing. Even the best of pleasures, such as the enjoyment of good music or literature, cannot go on indefinitely, for human resources are incapable of enjoying them without relaxation.

There may be no limit to our returning to them, but there is a limit to our staying with them.

> *More! More! is the cry of a mistaken soul:*
> *Less than all cannot satisfy Man.*
> —Blake

Your whole life is disordered and miserable if it is based on the principle of always having a good time, simply because happiness is a by-product, not a goal; it is the bridesmaid, not the bride; it flows from something else. You do not eat to be happy; you are happy because you eat. Hence, until you find out what your purpose in life is, you will never really have a good time.

Time is the greatest obstacle in the world to happiness, not only because it makes you take pleasures successively, but also because you are never really happy until you are unconscious of the passing of time! The more you look at the clock, the less happy you are! The more you enjoy yourself, the less conscious you are of the passing of time. You say, "Time passed like everything." Maybe, therefore, your happiness has something to do with the eternal! You can find happinesses in time, but what you want is Happiness that is timeless.

The other reaction to disappointment is much more reasonable. It begins by asking: "Why am I disappointed"; and then, "How can I avoid it?"

Why are you disappointed? Because of the tremendous disproportion between your desires and your realizations. Your soul has a certain infinity about it because it is spiritual; but your body and the world about you are material, limited, "cabined, cribbed, confined". You can imagine a mountain of gold, but you will never see one. You can imagine a castle of a hundred thousand rooms, one room studded with diamonds, another with emeralds, another with pearls, but you will never see such a castle.

In like manner, you look forward to some earthly pleasure or position or state of life, but, once you attain it, you begin to feel the tremendous disproportion between the ideal you imagined and the reality you possess. Disappointment follows. Every earthly ideal is lost by being possessed. The more material your ideal, the greater the disappointment; the more spiritual it is, the less the disillusionment. That is why those who dedicate themselves to spiritual interests, such as the pursuit of truth, never wake up in the morning with a dark brown taste in their mouths, or a feeling that they are run down at the heels.

Having discovered why you are disappointed, namely, because of the distance between an ideal conceived in the mind and its actualization in flesh or matter, you do not become a cynic. Rather, you take the next step of trying to avoid disappointments entirely. There is nothing abnormal about your wanting to live, not for two more years, but always; there is nothing strange about your desiring truth, not the truths of economics to the exclusion of history, but all truth; there is nothing inhuman about your craving for love, not until death do you part, not until satiety sets in or betrayal kills, but always.

Certainly you would never want this Perfect Life, Perfect Truth, and Perfect Love unless it existed? The very fact that you enjoy their fractions means there must be a whole. You would never know their arc unless there were a circumference; you would never walk in their shadows unless there were light.

Would a duck have the instinct to swim if there were no water? Would a baby cry for nourishment if there were no such thing as food? Would there be an eye unless there were Beauty to see? Would there be ears unless there were harmonies to hear? And would there be in you a craving for unending life, perfect truth, and ecstatic love unless Perfect Life and Truth and Love existed?

In other words, you were made for God. Nothing short of the Infinite satisfies you, and to ask you to be satisfied with less would be to destroy your nature. As great vessels, when launched, move uneasily on the shallow waters between the narrow banks of the rivers, so you are restless within the confines of space and time and at peace only on the sea of infinity.

Your mind, it would seem, should be satisfied to know one leaf, one tree, or one rose; but it never cries: "Enough." Your craving for love is never satisfied. All the poetry of love is a cry, a moan, and a weeping. The more pure it is, the more it pleads; the more it is lifted, above the earth, the more it laments. If a cry of joy and ravishment interrupts this plea, it is only for a moment, as it falls back again into the immensity of desires. You are right in filling the earth with the chant of your heart's great longing, for you were made for love.

No earthly beauty satiates you either for, when beauty fades from your eyes, you revive it, more beautiful still in your imagination. Even when you go blind, your mind still presents its image before you, without fault, without limits, and without shadow. Where is that ideal beauty of which you dream? Is not all earthly loveliness the shadow of something infinitely greater? No

wonder Virgil wished to burn his Aeneid and Phidias
wanted to cast his chisel into the fire. The closer they
got to beauty, the more it seemed to fly from them, for
ideal beauty is not in time but in the infinite.

Despite your every straining to find your ideals satisfied here below, the infinite torments you. The splendor of an evening sun as it sets like a "host in the golden
monstrance of the west", the breath of a spring wind,
the divine purity in the face of a Madonna, all fill you
with a nostalgia, a yearning, for something more beautiful still.

With your feet on earth, you dream of Heaven; creature of time, you despise it; flower of a day, you seek
to eternalize yourself. Why do you want Life, Truth,
Beauty, Goodness, and Justice, unless you were made
for them? Whence come they? Where is the source of
light in the city street at noon? Not under autos, buses,
or the feet of trampling throngs because there light is
mingled with darkness. If you are to find the source of
light, you must go out to something that has no admix-
ture of darkness or shadow, namely, to pure light, which
is the sun.

In like manner, if you are to find the source of Life,
Truth, and Love, you must go out to a Life that is not
mingled with its shadow, death, to a Truth not mingled
with its shadow, error, and to a Love not mingled with
its shadow, hate. You go out to something that is Pure
Life, Pure Truth, Pure Love, and that is the definition

of God. And the reason you have been disappointed is because you have not yet found Him!

If there had anywhere appeared in space
Another place of refuge where to flee,
Our hearts had taken refuge in that place,
And not with Thee.

For we against creation's bars had beat
Like prisoned eagles, through great worlds had
* sought*
Though but a foot of ground to plant our feet,
Where Thou wert not.

And only when we found in earth and air,
In heaven or hell, that such might nowhere be—
That we could not flee from Thee anywhere,
We fled to Thee.
                    —Richard Chenevix Trench

It is God for Whom we are looking. Your unhappiness is not due to your want of a fortune, or high position, or fame, or sufficient vitamins; it is due not to a want of something *outside* you, but to a want of something *inside* you. You cannot satisfy a soul with husks! If the sun could speak, it would say that it was happy when shining; if a pencil could speak, it would say that it was happy when writing—for these were the purposes for which they were made. You were made for perfect happiness. That is your purpose. No wonder everything short of God disappoints you.

But have you noticed that when you realize you were made for Perfect Happiness, how much less disappointing the pleasures of earth become? You cease expecting to get silk purses out of sows' ears. Once you realize that God is your end, you are not disappointed for you put no more hope in things than they can bear. You cease looking for first-rate joys where only tenth-rate pleasures are to be found.

You begin to see that friendship, the joys of marriage, the thrill of possession, the sunset and the evening star, masterpieces of art and music, the gold and silver of earth, the industries and the comforts of life, are all the gifts of God. He dropped them on the roadway of life, to remind you that if these are so beautiful, then what must be Beauty! He intended them to be bridges to cross over to Him. After enjoying the good things of life, you were to say: "If the spark of human love is so bright, then what must be the Flame!"

Unfortunately, many become so enamored of the gifts the great Giver of Life has dropped on the roadway of life that they build their cities around the gift, and forget the Giver; and when the gifts, out of loyalty to their Maker, fail to give them perfect happiness, they rebel against God and become cynical and disillusioned.

Change your entire point of view! Life is not a mockery. Disappointments are merely markers on the road of life, saying: "Perfect happiness is not here." Every disillusionment, every blasted earthly hope, every frustrated carnal desire, points to God. You can come to God not only by being good, but, if you only knew it, by a succession of disgusts.

The very sense of loss you feel in this world is in itself a proof that once you were possessed, and possessed by God. Though your *passions* may have been satisfied, *you* were never satisfied because while your passions can find satisfaction in this world, you cannot. If at the present time your vices have left you, do not think that you have left your vices.

Start with your own insufficiency and begin a search for perfection. Begin with your own emptiness and seek Him who can fill it. But you must be aware of your loneliness and want and disappointment before you can want Him to supply it. "Seek, and you shall find" (Mt 7:7).

Look at your heart! It tells the story of why you were made. It is not perfect in shape and contour, like a Valentine heart. There seems to be a small piece missing out of the side of every human heart. That may be to symbolize a piece that was torn out of the Heart of Christ which embraced all humanity on the Cross.

I think the real meaning is, that when God made your human heart, He found it so good and so lovable that He kept a small sample of it in Heaven. He sent the rest of it into this world to enjoy His gifts, and to use them as stepping stones back to Him, but to be ever mindful that you can never love anything in this world with your whole heart because you have not a whole heart with which to love. In order to love anyone with your whole heart, in order to be really peaceful, in order to be really whole-hearted, you must go back again to God to recover the piece He has been keeping for you from all eternity!

CHAPTER TWO

What Is God Like?

How do you think of God? Do you think of God as Someone on a throne who sulks and pouts and becomes angry if you do not worship and glorify Him? Do you think you make Him unhappy when you do not give Him attention, or do you imagine Him as One who will punish you if you do not praise Him, or go to church?

Or do you think of God as a benevolent grandfather who is indifferent to what you do; who likes to see you go places and do things, and does not care whether you have a good time by doing good things, or a good time by doing bad things, so long as you enjoy your-selves? Do you think of God in time of crisis as a vague ideal or a morale builder; and in time of peace as a silent partner whose name helps draw trade, but who has nothing to say about how the business shall be conducted?

If you hold either of these two views of God, you cannot understand either why you should worship God, or how God can be good if He does not let you do as you please.

Let us start with the first difficulty: *Why worship God?*

The word, "worship", is a contraction of "worth-ship". It is a manifestation of the worth in which we hold another person. Worship is a sign of value, the price we put on a service or a person. When you applaud an actor on the stage, or a returning hero, you are "worshipping" him in the sense of putting a value on his worth. Every time a man takes off his hat to a lady, he is "worshipping" her. Now to worship God means to acknowledge in some way His Power, His Goodness, and His Truth.

If you do not worship God, you worship something, and nine times out of ten it will be yourself. If there is no God, then you are a god; and if you are a god and your own law and your own creator, then we ought never to be surprised that there are so many atheists.

The basic reason there is so little worship of God today is because man denies he is a creature. Without a sense of creatureliness, or dependence, there can be no worship. But we have not yet answered the question "Why should you worship God?" You have a duty to worship God, not because He will pout and be imperfect and unhappy if you do not, but because if you do not worship God *you* will be imperfect and unhappy.

If you are a father, do you not like to receive a tiny little gift, such as a penny cigar, from your boy? Why do you value it more than a box of Corona Coronas from your insurance agent? If you are a mother, does not your heart find a greater joy in a handful of yellow dandelions from your little daughter than in a bouquet of roses from a dinner guest?

Do these trivialities make you richer? Do you need them? Would you be imperfect without them? They are absolutely of no utility to you! Yet you love them. Why? Because your children are "worshipping" you; because they are acknowledging your love, your goodness, and by doing so they are perfecting themselves, that is, developing along the lines of love rather than hate, thankfulness rather than ingratitude, and service rather than disloyalty. They are becoming more perfect children and more happy children.

As you do not need dandelions and chocolate cigars, neither does God need your worship. If their giving is a sign of your worth in your children's eyes, then are not prayer, adoration, and worship a sign of God's worth in our eyes? If you do not need your children's worship, why do you think God needs yours? If their worship is for *their* perfection, not yours, then may not your worship of Him be not for His perfection, but yours? Worship is your opportunity to express devotion, dependence, and love, and in doing that you make yourself happy.

A lover does not give gifts to the beloved because she is poor; he gives gifts because she is already in his eyes possessed of all gifts. The more he loves, the poorer he thinks his gifts are. If he gave her a million, he would still think he had fallen short. If he gave everything, even that would not be enough. One of the reasons he takes price tags off his gifts is not because he is ashamed, but because he does not wish to establish a proportion between his gift and his love. His gifts do not make her more precious, but they make him less inadequate. By giving, he is no longer nothing. The gift is his perfection, not hers. Worship in like manner is our perfection, not God's.

To refuse to worship is to deny a dependence that makes us independent. Worship is to us what blooming is to a rose. To refuse worship would be like the rose cutting itself off from the sun and the earth, or a student denying that history can teach him anything. To withhold admiration from one who deserves it is a sign of a jealous, conceited mind.

Every man who refuses to worship God is a social climber who wants to sit on God's throne and thus become hateful and mean because of a terrible inferiority complex: he knows down deep in his creature-heart that he is not a Creator, and that he could not be godless if there were no God. The man who is irreligious is like the man who is ignorant: both are imperfect, one in relation to his intellect, the other in relation to his whole being and his happiness.

God made you to be happy. He made you for your happiness, not His. God would still be perfectly happy if you never existed. God has no need of your love for His sake for there is nothing in you, of and by yourself, which makes you lovable to God. Most of us are fortunate to have even a spark of affection from our fellow creatures.

God does not love us for the same reason that we love others. We love others because of need. Our need of love is born of our poverty. We find in someone else the supply of our lack. But God does not love us because He needs us. He loves us because He put some of His love in us. God does not love us because we are valuable; we are valuable because He loves us.

Everybody feels he is envalued by love. "Nobody loves me" is the equivalent of being valueless. It is love that confers value, and the more important the person who loves you, the more precious is your value. You are infinitely precious because you are loved by God, but God is not infinite because you love Him.

God thirsts for you, not because you are His waters of everlasting life, but because you are the thirst, He the waters. He needs you only because you need Him. Without Him you are imperfect; but without you He is Perfect. It is the echo that needs the Voice, and not the Voice that needs the echo. "In this is charity: not as though we had loved God, but because he hath first loved us, and sent his Son to be a propitiation for our sins" (1 Jn 4:10).

Never think that, in giving glory to God, you are giving something without which He would be unhappy, and with which He becomes a dissatisfied dictator.

What is glory? Glory is *clara notitia cum laude*: a clear understanding of the worth of another which prompts us to praise. Glory is the result of knowledge and love.

When you are intensely interested in a subject, you love to talk about it: "Out of the abundance of the heart the mouth speaketh." Parents never tire of enthusing about their children. In like manner, a soul that knows God is his Creator, thinks about God, loves Him, and knows Him to be "so good" cannot keep the good news to himself. The overflow of human love for Divine Love is what is meant by giving glory to God.

Notice how it differs from publicity. Publicity is artificial stimulation. It is the attribution of worth to those who have either not earned it, or who have no right to it. Film stars need publicity agents, as toothpaste needs advertising. But did you ever hear of an American hero who needed a press agent? Praise is a by-product of his worth. The hero has worth.

Publicity tries to create worth; glory recognizes it. Publicity is the rouge on the anemic cheek of ordinariness; glory is the bloom that is the sign of health. The Church is not a publicity mill for drumming up trade for God's glory; it is a place where those who already know God's worth go to glorify Him.

Now we come to that other misunderstanding concerning God, the one that interprets His Goodness as indifference to justice and regards Him less as a loving father than as a doting grandfather who likes to see His children amuse themselves even when they are breaking things, including His commandments.

Too many assume that God is good only when He gives us what we want. We are like children who think our parents do not love us because they do not give us revolvers, or because they make us go to school. In order to understand goodness, we must make a distinction between getting what we *want* and getting what we *need*.

Is God good when He fulfills our wishes, or when we fulfill His? Is God good only when He gives us what we want, or is He good when He gives us what we *need* even though we do not want it?

When the prodigal son left the Father's house, he said: "Give me." He judged his father's goodness by the way the father satisfied his wants. But when he returned a much wiser young man, he merely asked for what he *needed*: a restoration of a father's love; and, hence, he said: "Make me."

The thief on the left judged the goodness of Our Lord by His power to take him down from his cross; that is what he *wanted*. The thief on the right judged the goodness of Our Lord by His power to take him into Paradise; that is what he *needed*.

The multitude in the desert were not given gold bricks or jewels or money by Our Divine Lord, and if they had been given, no one would have said that he had enough. But He gave them bread, and the Scriptures added "each one had his fill." That was what they needed.

The Goodness of God means that God gives us what we *need* for our perfection, not what we *want* for our pleasure and sometimes for our destruction. As a sculptor, He sometimes applies the chisel to the marble of our imperfect selves and knocks off huge chunks of selfishness that His image may better stand revealed. Like a musician, whenever He finds the strings too loose on the violin of our personality, He tightens them even though it hurts, that we may better reveal our hidden harmonies.

As the Supreme Lover of our soul, He does care how we act and think and speak. What father does not want to be proud of his son? If the father speaks with authority now and then to his son, it is not because he is a dictator, but because he wants him to be a worthy son. Not even progressive parents, who deny discipline and restraint, are indifferent to the progress of their children. So long as there is love, there is necessarily a desire for the perfecting of the beloved.

That is precisely the way God's goodness manifests itself to us. God really *loves* us and, because He loves us, He is not disinterested. He no more wants you to be unhappy than your own parents want you to be unhappy. God made you not for His happiness, but for yours, and to ask God to be satisfied with most of us as we really are, is to ask that God cease to love.

God could never let you suffer a pain or a reversal, or experience sadness, if it could not in some way minister to your perfection. If He did not spare His own Son on the Cross for the redemption of the world, then you may be sure that He will sometimes not spare your wants, that you might be all you *need* to be: happy and perfect children of a loving Father. He may even permit us to wage wars as a result of our selfishness, that we may learn there is no peace except in Goodness and Truth.

Most of us creatures must be a horror to God though we delude ourselves that we are really good. We judge ourselves by our neighbor, and say we cannot be so bad because our neighbor is worse. A painting may look good under the candlelight, but under the sun it is revealed as a daub. That is just what many of us must be in God's eyes. Think of the thousands you have met whom you could never love. You may even wonder how their mothers could love them, yet God loves them. He even loves them more than He loves us who look down on them with disdain and scorn.

If you want to know about God, there is only one way to do it: get down on your knees. You can make His acquaintance by investigation, but you can win His love only by loving. Arguments will tell you God exists for God's existence can be proved by reason; but only by surrender will you come to know Him intimately. A little study will tell you that your food must contain vitamins, as a little study will tell you that God created you. If, however, you do not eat vitamins once you know the necessity of vitamins, you may eventually lose your health. Likewise, if you do not love God Whom your reason proves to you, you may lose even your little knowledge.

That is one of the reasons why so many professors in secular institutions have no religion. They know about God, but they do not know God. It is one thing to know that your mother exists, it is another thing to love her. God, to these professors, is a theory, or a regulative principle of their thinking, or a final end to human aspirations, but no more. Because they do not *love* what they already know, because they do not act on their belief, even the little they have is taken away. They rattle the milk cans, but they never drink the milk.

As St. Paul told the Romans: "Because that, when they knew God, they have not glorified him as God, or given thanks; but became vain in their thoughts, and their foolish heart was darkened" (Rom 1:21). Most people who deny God do not do so because their reason tells them there is no God, for how could reason witness against Reason? Their denial is rather because of "wishful thinking". They feel they would be happier if there were no God, for then they could do as they pleased. Atheism, nine times out of ten, is born from the womb of a bad conscience. Disbelief is born of sin, not of reason.

Worship God because He is your perfection, more than knowledge is the perfection of the mind. Love Him because you cannot be happy without Love. Love Him quite apart from all you are, for you have the right to love Him in your heart, even though you do not always succeed in loving Him in your acts. Think a little less about whether you deserve to be loved by Him; He loves you even though you are not deserving. It is His love alone that will make you deserving. Most of us are unhappy because we never give God a chance to love us; we are in love only with ourselves. Say to yourself over and over again regardless of what happens: "God loves me!" And then add: "And I will try to love Him!"

CHAPTER THREE

What Are You Like?

Thus far we have answered two questions: Why were you made?, and What is God like? Now we ask: What are you like?

Take your heart into your hand as a kind of crucible and distill out of it its inmost nature. What do you find it to be? Are you not really a bundle of contradictions? Is there not a disparity between what you *ought* to do, and what you actually do? Do you not sometimes feel like a radio tuned into two separate stations, Heaven and hell, getting neither but only static and confusion worse confounded?

The old Latin poet Ovid expressed your sentiments perfectly when he said: "I see and approve the better things of life, the worse things of life I follow." St. Paul, too, expressed your inmost moods when he cried out: "For the good which I will, I do not; but the evil which I will not, that I do" (Rom 7:19).

You feel dual, divided against yourself because you more often choose what you like, rather than what is best for you. When you do, you always feel the worse for it. Somehow, within you there is a "kink"; your human nature is disorganized. You feel frustrated; your realizations are anticlimaxes; they turn out to be the opposite of what you expected. You are a problem to yourself, not because of your more obvious faults but because the better part of you so often goes wrong.

Your soul is the battlefield of a great civil war. The law of your members is fighting against the law of your mind. Your name is "legion"—you have no unifying purpose in life; there is only a succession of choices, but there is no one overall goal to which everything is subordinated. You are split into many worlds: eyes, ears, heart, body, and soul. In your more honest moments you cry out:

> *Within my earthly temple there's a crowd:*
> *There's one of us that's humble, one that's proud;*
> *There's one that's broken-hearted for his sins*
> *And one who unrepentant sits and grins;*
> *There's one who loves his neighbor as himself,*
> *And one who cares for naught but fame and pelf.*
> *From much corroding care I should be free,*
> *If once I could determine which is me.*
> —From "Mixed", *A Little Brother of the Rich,*
> *and Other Verses*, by Edward Sanford Martin
> (Charles Scribner's Sons)

How to explain this basic contradiction within you? There are four false explanations: psychological, biological, intellectual, and economic.

The psychological explanation attributes this tension within you to something peculiar to you as an individual—for example, to your erotic impulses, perhaps because you were frightened by a mouse in a dark closet during a thunderstorm while reading a book on sex.

This hardly fits the facts, because you are not the only one who is "that way"; everyone is. There is nothing strange about *you*. But there is something strange about *human nature*. Do not think that basically you are any different from anyone else in the world, or that you have a monopoly on temptations, or that you alone find it hard to be good, or that you alone suffer remorse when you do evil. It is human nature that is strange, not you.

The second false explanation is biological: the kink in your nature is due to a fall in evolution.

No! *Evil is not due to the animal in you.* Your human nature is very different from the animal's. There is a great discontinuity between a beast and a human. As Chesterton says: "You never have to dig very deep to find the record of a man drawing a picture of a monkey, but no one has yet dug deep enough to find the record of a monkey drawing the picture of a man."

An animal cannot sin since it cannot rebel against its nature. He *must* follow it. We can sin since we merely *ought* to follow our nature. When you see a monkey acting crazily in a zoo, throwing banana peels at spectators, you never say: "Don't be a nut." When, however, you see a man acting unreasonably, you say: "Don't be a monkey." Man alone can be subhuman; he can sink to the level of a beast.

The peculiar thing about a man is that, though he may cease to act like a man, he never loses the imprint of human dignity. The Divine image with which he was stamped is never destroyed; it is merely defaced. Such is the essence of a man's tragedy. We did not evolve from the beast; we devolved to the beast. We did not rise from the animal; we *fell* to the animal. That is why unless the soul is saved, nothing is saved. Evil in us presupposes what it defaces. As we never can be godless without God, so we never could be inhuman without being human.

The third false explanation attributes the evil in you to want of education: you are perverse because you are ignorant. Once you are educated, you will be good.

No! You do not have this inner contradiction because you lack knowledge, for the educated are not all saints and the ignorant are not all devils. Enlightenment does not necessarily make you better. Never before in the history of the world was there so much education, and never before was there so little coming to the knowledge of the truth. Much of modern education is merely a rationalization of evil. It makes clever devils instead of stupid devils. The world is not in a muddle because of stupidity of the intellect, but because of perversity of the will. We know enough: it is our choices that are wrong.

Finally, the socialist explanation of this tension, namely, people are wicked because they are poor, does not explain the facts.

Never before were living standards so high. All the rich are not virtuous, and all the poor are not wicked. If you had all the money in the world, you would still have that bias toward evil. If poverty were the cause of evil, why is it that juvenile delinquency increases in periods of prosperity and why does religion prosper in the vow of poverty? If poverty were the cause of evil, then riches should be the source of virtue. If that is so, why are not the wealthy the paragons of virtue?

The world has not just made a few mistakes in book-keeping that any expert accountant or economic advisor can correct; rather the world has swindled the treasury of faith and morality. It is not the world's arithmetic that is incorrect; it is our morals that are bad.

Since this perversion of human nature is universal, that is, since it affects human nature (not just your personality exclusively or mine), it must be due to something that happened to human nature itself at its very origin.

Secondly, since it is not animal in its origin, but has all the earmarks of being deliberate and the result of a free choice, it must not be a part of God's original work, but it must have come into being through some tendency to evil.

Thirdly, since evil is not merely a by-product of bad environment, but is endemic in the heart of man, it cannot be explained except on the basis of a universal fracture of some great moral law to which we are all bound.

Some acts of disobedience can be remedied. If I throw a stone through a window, I can put in a new one. But there are other kinds of disobedience that are irremediable, for example, drinking poison. Since evil is so universal in the world it must be due to a disobedience of the second kind and thus affects us in our inmost nature.

Either God created you the way you are now, or else you are fallen from the state in which God created you. The facts support the second view: the present tension and inner contradiction within us is due to some fault subsequent to the creation of human nature.

An unequivocal voice in your moral consciousness tells you that your acts of wrongdoing are abnormal facts in your nature. They ought not to be. There is something wrong inside of us. God made us one way; we made ourselves, in virtue of our freedom, another way. He wrote the drama; we changed the plot. You are not an animal that failed to evolve into a human; you are a human who rebelled against the Divine. If we are a riddle to ourselves, the blame is not to be put on God, but on us.

The fact remains: whatever you are, you are not what you ought to be. You are not a depraved criminal, but you are weak; you are not a mass of irremediable corruption, for you bear within yourself the image of God. You are like a man fallen into a well. You know you ought not to be there, and you know you cannot get out by yourself.

This is a roundabout way of saying that you need religion, but not a religion with pious platitudes. You want healing; you want deliverance; you want liberation. You know very well that there are a thousand things in your life that you thank God have not been found out by man. You want to get rid of these things. You do not want a religion to cheer you up on the roadway of life regardless of which road you take.

Analyzing your soul you discover it to be like an automobile that has run out of gas, and you are not quite sure of the right road. Hence, you need someone not only to give you some fuel for your tank, but also someone to point out your destination. If you have no religion at the present time, it may be because you rightly reacted against those bland assumptions that a few moral exhortations on Sunday will transform the world into the Kingdom of God.

You want a religion that starts, not with how good you are, but with how confused you are. Conscious as you are of being in bondage to perverted desires, selfishness, and churlish refusal to help someone in need, you cry out with the poet: "O my offense is rank; it smells to heaven."

You can love the lovable without being religious; you can respect those who respect you without religion; you can pay debts without being religious, but you cannot love those who hate you without being religious; you cannot atone for your guilty conscience without being religious.

Possibly the only reason in the world for loving the unlovely, for forgiving the enemy, is that God is love; and since as such He loves me who am so little deserving of His love, I also ought to love those who hate me.

The more you look into your soul, the more you see how false are the two modern views of human nature. Here in the liberal Western World we hear it said that we are naturally good and progressive, and, thanks to evolution, science, and inevitable progress, we are destined to become better and better until we become a kind of god. Two world wars in twenty-one years and the fear of a third knocks that false optimism into a cocked hat.

On the other hand, you know that the totalitarian views of Nazism, Fascism, and Communism are wrong for they assume that the individual man is intrinsically corrupt and can be made tame, docile, and obedient only by the force of the collectivity enshrined in a dictator.

The true view of human nature lies somewhere in between the two extremes of absolute goodness and total depravity—between optimism and pessimism. Your experience tells you that you are not a saint, but it also tells you that you are not a devil. The tendency toward evil in you is not an irremediable flaw, but an accident that can be controlled.

You feel like a fish on top of the Empire State Building; somehow or other you are outside of your environment. You cannot swim back, but Someone could put you back. You feel yourself like a clock that has all the works and still will not "go", because you have broken a mainspring. You cannot supply the new mainspring. The original Watchmaker could supply it, by sending His Son. Somewhere along the line, human nature became bungled, and it has all the earmarks of having been upset by a false use of freedom.

When you buy an automobile, the manufacturer gives you a set of instructions. He tells you the pressure to which you ought to inflate your tires, the kind of oil you ought to use in the crankcase, and the proper fuel to put in the gas tank. He has nothing against you by giving you these instructions as God had nothing against you in giving you commandments. The manufacturer wants to be helpful; he is anxious that you get the maximum utility out of the car. And God is anxious that we get the maximum happiness out of life. Such is the purpose of His commandments.

We are free. We can do as we please. We *ought* to use gas in the tank, but if we please, we can put in Chanel

Number 5. Now there is no doubt that it is nicer for our nostrils to fill the tank with perfume rather than with gasoline, but the car simply will not run on Smell Number 5. In like manner, we were made to run on the fuel of God's love and commandments, and we simply will not run on anything else. We just bog down.

CHAPTER FOUR

How You Got That Way

Anyone who gives freedom to another assumes great risks. A father yearns for the day when his son will be independent and able to make his own decisions. That hope is not without its fears, for freedom can be used either for weal or for woe. In a certain sense, even God took a great risk when He made man free, for the very freedom to become a son of the Eternal Father implied the possibility of becoming a rebel.

If God did not want to run that risk, there was still one other possibility. He might have made us like stones and stars, ice and hail, that is, good with the same necessity that the sun rises in the east and sets in the west.

What glory would there be in a universe wherein each element was a glittering diamond, but without the capacity to love? Is it any impeachment of God that He did not care to reign over an empire of stones? If He has deliberately set His children beyond mechanical control so that they could freely break allegiance with Him, was it not in order that there might be meaning and glory in the allegiance, when they freely choose to give it?

Instead, therefore, of making a universe wherein everything *must* act according to its nature, God made one in which one creature, man, merely *ought* to act according to his nature. In other words, He made a moral universe, a vale of character-making wherein there would be virtue, heroism, saintliness, and patriotism, none of which is possible without freedom.

Fire is never praised for being hot, nor ice for being cold. But men are praised for being virtuous, because they could have been vicious; they are lauded for being heroes, because they could have been cowards; and they are extolled for being saints, because they might have been devils.

God chose, therefore, to make a moral universe, but morality is impossible without freedom. Since He made us free to choose what is right, we are also free to choose the wrong. The eternal idea of Justice makes no one just, as the eternal Right makes no one righteous. In a certain sense, we are less free than freeable; we make ourselves free. Before truth and righteousness and freedom can become mature, they require training, discipline, trial, and the awful possibility of failing.

The whole purpose of education is to train minds to use freedom rightly. We do not take away the freedom of youths because they might abuse it. Hence, parents offer encouragement, reward, or praise to their children in order that they might choose the good rather than the evil. This is what God did at the very beginning. He did not give man the frightening responsibilities of freedom without at the same time offering him incentives to choose right rather than wrong. God would not force His happiness on anyone.

Regardless of how much you liked ice cream, you would not enjoy it if it were forced down your throat. You will never be happy doing things unless you want to do them. Hence, God gave man a free will with which he might choose the things he liked, rather than be forced to accept them. As freedom implies choice, so choice implies alternatives. So, God gave our first parents a choice.

In almost so many words, God said to Adam and Eve at the very beginning of history: As an inducement to choose what is best, I shall give you certain gifts. If you use your freedom in the direction of what is best for you, that is, for your perfection, I shall give you permanently the supernatural gift of sharing in My Nature, that is, being a child of God and an heir of Heaven. To this I add permanently some lesser gifts: You will never die, your passions will never rebel against your reason, and your mind will be exempt from error.

What is rather difficult to understand here is the word, "supernatural". What does it mean? A stone is not constructed so as to grow. That is simply not its nature. But if the stone in your back yard suddenly began to bloom, you would say it was possessed of supernatural powers. It would have done something which does not belong to the powers, the capacities or the nature of a stone.

In like manner, if the flower in your garden suddenly began to walk, and to get out of the rain, and to smell other flowers, and to move to Florida or California in the winter, it would be something supernatural for the flower, something above and beyond its capacity and its needs. In order to do these things some new element and power would have to be added to the flower. So, too, if your dog began to quote Shakespeare, to read the market quotations, and to build its own doghouse, you would conclude that something *above* and beyond the nature of a dog had been given to it.

By nature, that is, naturally, we are just creatures of God's handiwork. We are not, in the strict sense of the term, God's children; we are only God's creatures. But suppose God gave us the power of being His children, of sharing His Divine Life, of being a member of the family of the Trinity, of being heirs of Heaven—that would be supernatural for us, more supernatural than for a marble to sprout, and for a rose to write music, or for a dog to speak.

To preserve these gifts for themselves and posterity, one condition was imposed by God, on Adam and Eve, and it was very easy. They merely had to love God, Who is their perfection. We must not think that this condition was equivalent to saying to a child: "If you eat a woolly worm, I will give you a dollar", because a woolly worm is not the perfection of a child. Rather, it was like saying to the child: "If you drink milk and eat vitamins, you will be healthy." As obeying the laws of health is the perfection of the child, so, too, obeying the will of God is our perfection.

We said that the one condition imposed was that they love God. But how could man prove his love of God? How do you know anyone loves you? Because he tells you? Not necessarily. Love proves itself less by words than by an act of choice. Human love is not love unless it is free; it is only because of the possibility of saying "No" that there is so much charm in the "Yes". Love is not only an affirmation; it is also a negation. When a husband chooses a wife, he not only accepts one woman, he excludes as wife every other woman in the world.

Our first parents were told that they must prove their love of God by an act of choice. This implied an alternative. The alternative was a choice between a fruit and a garden, the part and the whole. God said they could eat of all the fruits in the garden of Paradise, save the tree of knowledge of good and evil.

Was there anything unreasonable about the trial? Is not life filled with abundant instances of receiving rewards on the condition of love? Imagine a wealthy man going away for the summer and telling the chauffeur and his wife that they may live in his house, eat his food, drink his wine, use his cars, and ride his horses, but on one condition: that they must not eat the artificial apple he has on the dining room table. The owner well knows the artificial apple will give them indigestion. He does not tell them that. They ought to trust him in the light of all he has done for them.

If the wife persuades her husband to eat the apple, she would not be a lady; and if he eats it, he would not be a gentleman. By doing the one thing forbidden, they would lose all the good things provided and have indigestion besides, and they even lose the opportunity of passing these things on to their children.

To make light of the apple in the story of the Fall is to miss the point that it was the test of love. Not to shake hands with a passerby on the street is of no importance, but not to shake hands as a sign of contempt is very serious. Eating of the forbidden fruit was a sign of contempt: the symbol of rebellion. God was imposing a single limit to the sovereignty of man, reminding him that if he did the one thing forbidden, he would imperil all the things provided. Like Pandora, he opened the forbidden box, and he lost all his treasures.

Test your own experience. Have you ever fallen? Have you ever sinned? Did anyone ever tempt you to sin against your true self? You never fell unless there was something that attracted, a whispered doubt, a lie, and a dream of being happier than you are now. Such elements were in the Fall.

Our parents were enjoying the happiness of a sinless Eden, but very soon Satan, a fallen angel, appeared and, pointing to the forbidden fruit, which was delightful to behold, whispered the first doubt. It began with a Why? "Why hath God commanded you that you should not eat of every tree of paradise?" (Gen 3:1). The evil behind the question was: God cannot be good if He does not let you do whatever you please. Freedom to Satan is the absence of law and restraint. Satan, the father of lies, was saying: "God is a Fascist."

Have you ever noticed that the first suggestion to do wrong always comes from someone who makes you think that you would be more free if you defied your conscience? Perhaps, if you are Catholic, they said to you: "Why does the Church forbid you to marry again? After all, you have your own life to lead." The approach is diabolically clever for it makes it appear that the Church is making you do something you do not want to do and therefore, is in some way restraining your liberty. Freedom, if we only knew it, is within the law of our nature, not outside it. Try to be so progressive and broadminded as to draw a giraffe with a short neck, or a triangle with four sides, and see where you end!

The second stage is ridicule. When Eve answered that it was God's command that they eat not the forbidden fruit, for, if they did, they would die, Satan ridiculed the idea: "You shall not die the death" (Gen 3:4). God has lied to you! It is stupid to believe such silly superstitions!

If you resisted for a time the temptation to divorce and to marry again, by saying: "No! The Church is Divine"; or, "I will lose my soul if I break the law of Christ: 'What God hath joined together let no man put asunder'", did not your tempter deny it laughingly: "Don't be silly! The Church is only one of the sects, and you are certainly not so medieval as to believe in a soul or a hell, are you?"

Finally, comes the third stage, the false promise. Eve dwelt jealously on the one thing forbidden, rather than the many things permitted, until quite unconsciously she was ready to be convinced that Satan's promise was true. "For God doth know that in what day soever you shall eat thereof, your eyes shall be opened: and you shall be as gods, knowing good and evil" (Gen 3:5).

The good she knows begins to pall, the evil she does not know begins to allure. More and more she turns from conscience to the imagined sweetness of the forbidden fruit. There would be but one result. They who would pluck flowers from the edge of the precipice must be prepared to fall. Swiftly the crisis is upon her, as all crises are. She eats the forbidden fruit and gives it to Adam to eat; then the floodgates are open, and the tiny ripple of an illicit thought, ever deepening, swelling, broadening, burst into an irresistible floodwater which engulfed the world.

Have you not done exactly the same thing when you fell? When you spoke of Christ's command forbidding marriage while the other spouse was living, did not your tempter respond with a false promise: "You will be very happy with your new spouse. He is just suited for you." Or, "You always needed a husband who could appreciate you." Then came the divorce, the remarriage, and the fall.

What is unnatural or unhistorical about the Fall of man? You, too, once had your Eden of happy ignorance, of innocence unassailed. Then your self-will asserted itself; your "mine" against the Divine "Thine". You interpreted freedom as the right to rebel, or the right to do whatever you *pleased*, instead of the right to do whatever you ought. You were like errant steam engines that refused to follow the tracks laid down by the Master Engineer; like golfers who refused to keep their heads down when they swung, and then blamed the clubs or the caddy master when they "dubbed" the shot; like copies that conspired to be originals; like adjectives that insisted on being nouns; like rays that claimed to be the sun; like printed pages that insisted you were the author.

All of these things you *can* do, because you are free, but when you do them, you really destroy your freedom. You are bulbs that can glow only when in contact with the Divine Energy; without it you are not really yourselves. Like campaign orators, you talked so much about freedom you lost your voices, and lost your freedom of speech.

When children, we were told not to play with matches. We disobeyed and burned ourselves. Then, when mother called, we hid. We had no fear of our mother before we burned ourselves, but only after. Adam had no fear of God before he disobeyed. After his sin, God seemed to be an angry God. To the bad conscience God appears always the God of wrath. The boy who broke the vase by throwing a ball at it, says to his mother: "Now Mummy, don't get mad." Anger is not in the mother; anger is in the boy's projection to his mother of his own sense of justice. Anger is not in God; anger is in our disordered selves.

You say: "Science has proven the Fall false!" Science has nothing to say about it, because science knows man only as he is now. Because we can no longer find the core of the fruit Adam ate does not prove that Adam never ate the fruit, any more than, because we cannot find the remains of Christ, it follows that Christ never died.

"How could physical science prove that man was not depraved? You do not cut open a man to find his sins. You do not boil him until he gives forth the unmistakable green fumes of depravity. How could physical science find any traces of a moral fall? What traces does the scientist expect to find? Does he expect to find a fossil Eve with a fossil apple inside her? Did he suppose that the ages would have spared for him a complete skeleton of Adam attached to a slightly faded fig leaf?" (G. K. Chesterton, *All Things Considered*).

You say it is a myth? It is not! It is an historically revealed fact, verified by subsequent history and by the individual experience of man. It is an undeniable fact. You know very well that you ought to be an other-regarding creature, that your true happiness is in living for others. You also know that you are selfish, and you are weak and self-centered and sometimes hateful to yourself and others. God did not make you that way! You in some way have departed from your own true nature.

But you ask: "Well! Granted that Adam sinned! What have I to do with Adam? Why should I be punished because of him?" When Congress declared war on December 8, 1941, you declared war without any explicit declaration on your part. What Congress did, we did. Adam is the head of the human race. "By one man, sin entered the world" (Rom 5:12).

You say: "It was very unjust of God to deprive me of friendship with Him, and of these other gifts, simply because Adam sinned." There would have been injustice if God deprived you of your due, but you are no more entitled to be a child of God than a razor has a right to bloom, or a rose has the right to bark, or a dog has the right to quote Dante. What Adam lost was gifts, not a heritage.

On Christmas Day, when you distribute gifts to your friends, would I have a right to say to you: "Why do you not give me a gift?" You would answer: "I am not doing you an injustice, because I owe you nothing. I am not obliged to give these gifts to my friends. If

I had not given them gifts, I would not have deprived them of anything I owed them." So, neither did God owe us anything beyond our nature as a creature of His handiwork.

The loss of the supernatural gift of being a child of God weakened man's will and darkened his intellect without corrupting his nature. Here we must repeat: man's nature was not made intrinsically corrupt and wicked by the Fall. This is a caricature of the true doctrine. Original sin does not mean that we are born in the state we are in, but that through Adam we have fallen into that state.

The Fall disorganized man's normal human faculties, making him just as he is now, with a bias toward evil, with a will reluctant to do good, with a tendency to rationalize evil. But he is still man—not a depraved man, totally corrupt as those who ridicule the doctrine of the Fall say, but still a person able to recover part of his former gifts. The disorder in us is like getting dirt in our eyes: we still have the eye as an organ of sight, but it now sees through tears. The result is we are disorganized; suffering and pain came into life; women had to bear their children in sorrow, while men had to earn their bread by the sweat of their brow.

Because man turned his will against God, so now his passions and desires are turned against man's will. It is this fallen nature which all men have inherited. That is why the sin is called "original"—it came at the origin

of human nature, and represents a loss, the soul register-
ing a much greater loss than the body; for Man still has
natural life, but he has not supernatural life.

It is right here that Christianity begins. In all other
religions you have to be good to come to God. In Christianity you do not. Christianity is realistic: it begins with
the fact that, whatever you are, you are not what you
ought to be. If everything in the world were perfectly
good, we would still need God, for all goodness comes
from God. But the presence of evil makes that need
more imperative. Christianity begins with the recognition that there is something in your life and in the world
that *ought* not to be, that need not be, and that could be
otherwise were it not for evil choices.

Of course you can say: "I need no religion", for,
after all, if you are your own god, then you need no
other God to worship; if you are perfect, then no one
can make you better; if you know all Truth, then not
even God can teach you anything; if you have never
done wrong, then you need no Savior. It is wonderful
in these days of atheism to find so many people who
believe in god—I mean themselves.

If you are dissatisfied, unhappy, feel oppressed, are
weighed down with interior conflicts, neuroses, depres-
sions, and complexes; if guilt weighs upon your soul; if
you need the truth other than your own, and love other
than that of creatures, and life beyond that of horses;
if you know you are not intrinsically corrupt; if you

know that death is not a negligible incident in your life, that you cannot ignore suffering in yourself and others; if you know you cannot eliminate a self-rebuking conscience as a social illusion; if you know that you could be better than you are; if you feel like the master painting of a great artist that has become somewhat defaced and stained; if you know that you are too good for the rubbish heap, you are not too spoiled to hang in the Metropolitan Gallery; if you know that you cannot restore yourself to your pristine beauty; if you know that no one could restore you better than the Divine Artist who made you, then you have already taken the first step toward peace. Herein is the essence of Christianity. The Divine Artist did come to restore the original! That is the Good News!

CHAPTER FIVE

Who Can Remake You?

You remember the nursery rhyme:

> *Humpty Dumpty sat on the wall;*
> *Humpty Dumpty had a great fall;*
> *And all the King's horses and all the King's*
> *   men*
> *Could never put Humpty Dumpty together*
> *   again.*

That rhyme expresses the condition of human nature as a result of original sin; since the Fall man is like a broken egg. The tragedy of his condition is that neither he nor any natural agent can put him together again, and that he must do so if he is to fulfill the highest purpose of his existence. Man can remedy political and economic disorders, but not the disorder inside himself. He needs God for that; hence the greater necessity of religion.

It has been said that we are like a clock whose mainspring is broken. We have the "works", but we do not "go". In order to put the clock in condition, two conditions must be fulfilled: (1) The mainspring must be supplied from the outside; (2) It must be placed inside the clock. Man cannot redeem himself any more than the clock can fix itself. If man is ever to be redeemed, redemption must (1) Come from without; (2) Be done from within.

Why must salvation come from without? Because human nature has contracted a bigger debt than it can pay. In sinning against God, we piled up an infinite debt, and we have not enough balance of merits in our finite bank to meet the burden. We barely have enough merits to meet current expenses. We cannot depend upon time to blot out our sins, for time, instead of blotting out sin, adds to it.

Salvation must come from without because you can destroy life, but you cannot create it; you can blind your vision but you cannot restore it; you can destroy your communion with God by sin, but you cannot restore it. Press a rose petal between your fingers, and you can never restore its tint. Lift a dew drop from a leaf, and you can never replace it. Evil, in like manner, is too deep-seated in the world to be righted by a little kindness or reason and tolerance.

You might just as well tell a man suffering from gout that all he needed was to play six sets of tennis; or to tell a consumptive that all he needed was to take up long-distance running; or to tell a criminal that all he needed to make him a good citizen was to own a fine home with plumbing and electric lights. Man has radically failed. He cannot save himself.

The humanist experiment was tried for centuries. We need something more than the human to make us rightly human. Some intervention outside of the time-scheme is absolutely necessary. Some evil things we do are remediable, like a mistake in writing; we can turn over a new leaf. Other mistakes are irremediable, like losing a leg through carelessness.

Between God and us there is a wall. The avalanche of sin has fallen and blocked the roadway of life. He can get along without us, for He is absolutely independent of all outside causes; but we cannot get along without Him, for we are totally dependent on Him for all that we are.

Since we offended the dignity of the infinite God, our sin, in a way, becomes infinite, and calls for an infinite reparation. But we are finite. The sin does not work out. Hence, salvation must come from without. Our human will is too weak to conquer its own evil, as the sick may be too weak to cure their own disability. We heed a teacher for our minds, a physician for our bodies, and a Redeemer for our souls—a Redeemer from *without*: outside humanity with its weakness, its sin and its rebellion.

Though salvation must come from *without*, it, nevertheless, must be done from *within* humanity. It would do no good to the clock to put the mainspring inside a radio. If salvation were not done *inside* humanity, it would have no relation to humanity. If I were arrested for speeding, you could not go into the court room and say: "Try me instead of the guilty one." The judge would say: "What have you to do with the case?" There is no substitution in the eyes of the law. Furthermore, any man who is conscious of his guilt does not want to be "let off". It is not human pride, but a deep sense of justice and responsibility and dignity which makes us rebel against a pardon without satisfaction.

In our relations with our fellowmen, we often say: "I want to make up for it", and there is no reason why in our relation to God we should act any differently. Surely God could condone our guilt with a single act of His will. Forgiveness without reparation by the sinner would be immoral only if it meant ignoring guilt and sin, or if it belittled the eternal necessity of righteousness. But it seems proper that offending human nature be involved in its own redemption.

In order, therefore, that fallen man may be re-created, two conditions are essential:

1. Man must be redeemed from *without* because no man can lift himself by his own boot straps. Since the offense of man's sin is infinite, and the reparation he can make is only finite, it follows that it can be adequately done only by God.

2. Man must be redeemed from *within*, otherwise the
   redemption would have no relation to man, and
   man wants to play the role in his own regeneration. He does not merely want his sins forgiven; he
   wants to atone for them. To answer that need God
   becomes man.

Posit these two conditions, and you have the reason
why the Redeemer should be both God and man. He
should have the nature of God and the nature of man,
and the two should be united in the Person of God. In
that case, man could cooperate with God in his own
redemption.

Imagine a pencil on a table. That pencil has a nature;
and its nature is to write. Of and by itself it cannot write.
In like manner, man of and by himself cannot blot out
the infinite liability of his sin. Now, imagine another
nature, the nature of a hand coming down to that pencil. Here we have the union of two natures in a single
person which took up the pencil. The pencil is now
able to write—something which it could not do before
it was united with the nature of the hand.

When it does write, you do not say, the pencil writes,
or my fingers write, but you say: "I write." You attribute the action of the pencil to your person. So, too,
if God were to unite man to Himself, then man could
do things which of and by himself he could not do.
When that manhood which God assumed did anything,

for example, prayed, or breathed, or spoke, or suffered, its actions would be attributed to His Person. Since He is the Person of God, it would have infinite value. This is what happened in Bethlehem: God became man and appeared in history as Jesus Christ.

Jesus Christ is both God and man. He was God before He was man. He is God who became a man, not a man who became a god. The word, "Incarnation", means "in the flesh", and signifies that Christ is born not by the conversion of the Godhead into flesh, but by taking manhood into God. The Incarnation does not mean the beginning of a *new Person*. From all eternity He is the Person of God. All the Person of God had to do to become man was to assume a human nature. "In the beginning was the Word, and the Word was with God and the Word was God. And the Word was made flesh and dwelt among us" (Jn 1:1, 14).

Was His human nature like ours? Yes, in all things, save sin. He had to take His human nature from the very race that had fallen, in order that He might suffer and act as man. But His human nature could not be sinful like ours, otherwise He Himself would stand in need of Redemption, and "if the blind lead the blind, both fall into the pit" (Mt 15:14).

The problem was how to be a man like us, without being contaminated as we were, by sin. He could be a man like us by being born of woman. He could be a sinless man, or the new Adam, by being born of a

Virgin. By dispensing with the act of generation by
which original sin was propagated, He escaped its infec-
tion. That is why He was born of a Virgin. The Virgin
Birth broke the heritage of sin, as now for the first time
since Adam there walked on earth a human nature as
God meant it to be.

The Incarnation solved the problem that man ought
in justice make satisfaction for his sins, but only God *can*.
Out of pure love, therefore, God in Christ identified
Himself with humanity that He might make reparation
in its behalf. By becoming man, He stood on man's level.
Knowing no sin, He "became sin" in order to redeem.

Just as it would be foolish to tell a wife that she need
feel no shame because her husband had committed a
crime, so it would be foolish to tell Christ, the Incarnate
God, that He need feel no shame because He was per-
sonally guiltless.

Love means fellowship, not isolation. Human love
takes on the burden of its friends; Divine Love takes on
Himself the sins of the world. That is why, though sinless, He stood silent before the judges, for the sins of the
world were upon Him; that is why He who was guiltless
was baptized, that He might identify Himself with the
debt which all men owed. And the payment He made
was not an individual payment; it was a payment on
behalf of humanity whose very nature He shared.

The old human nature descended from Adam was
disordered; He would not take that upon Himself. So

the Holy Spirit created a perfectly new human nature in the womb of Mary, a new Adam, a new creature, a new pattern. God would not put a patch of holiness on the old garment of nature. He gave the human race a new start. Only by repeating in a way the act of creation, by making a new human out of the old, could God bring into the world a nature that could be called "a new creature". "Behold I make all things new" (Rev 21:5). With Him a new race was born out of the old race.

From the religious point of view the world is not divided into nations, races, or classes, but into two humanities: the old, unregenerate humanity under the headship of Adam; and the new, regenerated humanity under the headship of Christ. How do we become incorporated into each of these humanities? By being born. Being born of the flesh makes us members of the race of Adam; being born of the baptismal waters of the Holy Spirit makes us members of the race of Christ.

The only way this continued inheritance of original sin could be broken was by a direct act of the Creator Himself. Christ achieved the re-creation of man in His own Person; it remains for us to apply it to ourselves and through ourselves to the material universe, so that all things might be restored in Him. On the First Easter Sunday, the new humanity consisted of only one individual human being, Christ, as at Creation humanity consisted of only one individual person, Adam. By

His Incarnation, Christ restored in Himself fallen Adam with his descendants.

Hence, the essence of Christianity consists not in obeying a set of commands, nor in submitting to certain laws, nor in reading Scripture, nor in following the example of Christ. Before all else, it consists in being re-created, remade and incorporated into the risen Christ, so that we live His life, think His thoughts and will His Love.

Before studying the application of His Redemption, it is well to recall four important truths about the Person of Christ:

1. He is the only head of a religion in the world who had a pre-history. No one ever expected Buddha, or Confucius, or Mohammed, or any of the more recent founders of religion. But the whole world, both Jew and Gentile, did expect Christ. The place of His birth, the city in which He would dwell, the time of His coming, the manner of His death, all were foretold by the prophets of one particular nation whom God chose as His instrument for the redemption of man.

God had been in nature as *Providence*; He had been in history as *prophecy*; now, when the fullness of time is come, God appears in history as *man*. At a precise moment of human history, God cut into human processes by taking upon Himself a human nature in the womb of a Jewish maiden. Time was fashioned so as to receive Christ. History worked up to Him; history worked from Him. Through Him history has meaning and purpose. That is why all history is divided into B.C. and A.D.

2. He is not primarily a teacher of humanitarian ethics, but essentially and primarily a Redeemer and a Savior. Everyone else came into this world to live; He came into it to die. Death was a stumbling block to Socrates; to Christ it was the goal of His life, the very gold He was seeking. So long as God remained in the heavens, He was the object of intellectual scrutiny. Once He came down into the dust of human lives, He was in the domain of historical decision. Men could no longer be indifferent to Him.

Before He came, God was either known or unknown. When He came, He would be either passionately loved or passionately hated. One can never be indifferent before the Infinite. Death in a certain sense was inevitable, for once Love and Innocence confront brute force and sin, a crucifixion follows. Suffering is always the form that love takes in an evil situation. Every mother who ever had an erring son and every wife who ever had a drunkard husband know that. How else could Divine Love meet sin, except by a cross? Evil breaks some human hearts. Sin broke the heart of God. "Greater love than this no man hath, that a man lay down his life for his friends" (Jn 15:13).

3. Jesus Christ is both true God and true man. He is not only a good man. A good man never lies, but if Christ is not what He claimed to be, the Son of God, then He is the greatest liar of all times. A good man never deceives, but if Christ cannot give what He promised, namely, peace and pardon to our hungry tired souls, then He is the arch-deceiver of history. Either Christ is the Son of God, or He is antichrist. He is not just a good man. If He were only man, He, too, would need redemption. If He were only God, He could not redeem man; He could only forgive him.

The Redeemer of man was then both Divine and human; human that He might act in our name; Divine that His actions might have an infinite value. There are some who would say that He is the highest product of God in the whole history of the world, but that He is not God. This description does not fit Christ, God and man, though it does fit His Blessed Mother, for to her was given the power in the name of all humanity to accept the Incarnation of the Son of God as in the blazing light of her innocence she answered the angel: "Be it done unto me according to thy Word."

4. He was the new Adam. The human race, it has been said, has two heads: Adam and Christ. As all men are in Adam by the flesh; men can be in Christ by the Spirit. "For as by the disobedience of one man, many were made sinners; so also by the obedience of one,

many shall be made just" (Rom 5:19). The three instruments which cooperated in the Fall were: (a) a disobedient man: Adam; (b) a proud woman: Eve; (c) a tree. These three instruments were used by God in the re-creation of man: (a) for the disobedient Adam, there is the new obedient Adam, Christ; (b) for the proud woman, Eve, there is the humble Virgin Mary; (c) for the tree of Eden, the new tree of the Cross on Calvary.

How did this Redemption take place?

By the sinless being made sin. Our Blessed Lord, though He was sinless, nevertheless willed "to be made sin for us". As a strong magnet attracts to itself iron filings, so He by an act of His Will drew unto Himself all the sins of the world that have ever been committed, sins of Jews and Gentiles, sins too awful to be mentioned, sins too terrible to be named. He permitted them all to be thrust into His Hands, as if He Himself had committed them, and the very thought of them was so terrible that, one night in the Garden, His Blood poured out from His Body in a crimson sweat. The cup was bitter, but since the Father willed it, He would drink it to its very dregs.

By coming into a world of sin, He, the Sinless One, brought the whole weight of its sin upon His Person. As doctors who are free from disease will sometimes accept the possibility of contagion in their eagerness to cure their patients of a disease, so He, though sinless, freely accepted the cumulative weight of human transgression that He might atone for the very punishment which our sins deserved. It was faintly like a rich man who makes himself responsible for the debts of a bankrupt person so that he might start business all over again, except with Our Lord the cost was greater, namely, His life. Being God He became man that He might lay down His Life for us who were not His friends, but His enemies.

Imagine a golden chalice which has been consecrated for Divine worship and used on the altar at Mass. Suppose this chalice is stolen, mingled with alloys, and beaten down to a cigarette case. Later on, it is recovered. Before the gold of that chalice can be restored to the altar, it must first of all be subjected to purging fires to burn away the dross. It must be remolded by repeated blows of a hammer and then only may it be reconsecrated and restored to its dignity and honor.

Our human nature was like that battered and desecrated chalice, no longer serving the high purpose for which it was made. The chalice could not remake itself. Neither could man redeem himself. So Christ took upon Himself our human nature, plunged it into the flaming furnace of Calvary's fires that the dross of sin might be burned away. Then on Easter Sunday, by rising from the dead, He reversed the Fall, and appeared as the New Man, remolded and glorified, fit for God's service and restored to God's friendship.

The Easter Resurrection was the final proof that God's love in man and for man had won the final victory over sin and death. For the worst thing that sin could do is not to bomb cities and kill a fellowman; it is to crucify God. Having done this and lost, it would never do anything as bad again. Having been conquered at its strongest point, evil must now remain eternally defeated.

Christ had achieved the re-creation of man in His own person. He did not need this Redemption for Himself, but in His Divine Love of us He took upon Himself the burden of our human nature, that He might become the life-giving Form of redeemed humanity, or the Pattern of men to whom—"as many as are willing to receive Him"—He would give the power to become the sons of God.

All that remains to be done is for all mankind to appropriate this new life to itself. He was the beginning of a new coinage to take the place of the counterfeit. He was the original, the new die; millions and millions of worthy coins can be stamped from that die. Whether we do it and thus become regenerated depends on our will. He has vindicated the Divine Justice and the honor of God's Holiness, He has become the Life in and through which we may regain the heritage of the children of God; He has in His Sacred humanity re-created the immortal life out of morality.

Upright as a Priest on the Cross, prostrate as a Victim, He has brought man to God and God to man in Himself, that "we might have life and have it more abundantly", if we in our turn, will to be made conformable to Him in His Cross and Sacrifice. Such is the mystery of Calvary. "O Happy Fault, which has merited to have such and so great a Redeemer."

The two great truths we have learned so far and which stand in opposition to much contemporary rubbish and conform so well with the facts of human experience and history are:

Man did not come from the beast.

Christ did not come from humanity.

You did not come from the dogs, but you can go to the dogs; you did not evolve from the animal, but you can devolve to the animal. You are less a risen monkey than you are a fallen angel. You were once not lower than you are now; but you were once higher. You are more a disinherited king, than you are an enthroned beast; your golden age was more in the past, rather than in the next twenty years.

The same is true of the person of Christ. As you did not come from the animal, Christ did not come from history or from man alone. History did not beget Him as it begot Lincoln and Napoleon; rather He begot history. Through Him and Him alone, the history of nations and the history of each individual man find an absolute and unalterable center. Even though you ignore Him, even though you deny His existence, you must date your denial as over nineteen hundred years after His birth. [Bishop Sheen is writing in 1946.—ED.] He is the Supreme Reality of history, the cornerstone in the edifice of humanity, the keystone in the arch of time, and the measure of the world; the Lamb slain from the beginning of the world.

The title which He applied to Himself was that of the Good Shepherd who lays down His Life for His sheep. A careful study of the Gospel reveals that only through His suffering and death could the Kingdom of God be fully established and men reinstated under the authority of God. "If I be lifted up, I will draw all things to myself." Mankind had contradicted God, so He would die on the sign of contradiction, which is the Cross.

The Cross makes intelligible the gravity of human sin. Some say the only reason Christ went to the Cross was to show us that He loved us. If a man were sitting safely on a pier fishing and a good neighbor came up behind him, threw himself into the river and, as he went down for the third time, said: "This shows how much I love you", the whole ceremony would be ridiculous if it were not so tragic. But, if the fisherman had actually fallen into the river, and the good neighbor lost his life saving him, then we could say of him truly: "Greater love than this no man hath, that a man lay down his life for his friends" (Jn 15:13).

In like manner, the Cross is meaningful only because we are sinners, and the love of the Cross is manifest because He loved us while we were sinners. Though sinners brought upon Him all manner of torture, both physical and spiritual; though they lied and vilified Him; were treacherous and malicious, He went on loving them until the end when in a last and final moment He prayed: "Father, forgive them, for they know not what they do" (Lk 23:34). Sin had caused enmity between man and God; it had produced divisions and antagonisms between man and man, class and class, nation and nation. Now, through the Cross, He reconciles the world to God, making peace through His Death and restoring us in Him to the Fatherhood of God.

The Cross of Christ forces you to make up your mind. You can be indifferent about anything else, but you cannot be indifferent about the Crucifixion. You can stand immobile before a cross as a kind of charm, but you cannot help but feel involved when you look at a Crucifix. It is the one thing in the world that either makes you feel comfortable or uncomfortable. It never leaves you detached. It challenges you to say one of two things: either to say a firm, unshakable *Yes* to the proposition that God is love, or else a hoarse, derisive *No* to the proposition that the maximal point of devotion and love is a snare and a delusion.

So compelling is the response one way or the other, that you cannot refer the Crucifixion either to history alone, or to the community alone, or to the Jews alone, or to the Romans or the Greeks. It has an individual reference as well as a cosmic reference. Each heart must answer it for himself. Try as much as you can you cannot stand before that Crucifixion and shout: "No! I will not have this man's reign over me." Like the

"Amen" that stuck in the throat of Macbeth, the words will stick in your own throat. Your own heart gives the lie to your lips that say: "This is not Love!" Your flesh may be unwilling, but your spirit cries out: "Here is One to Whom I ought to commit my life." If you are willing to do that, another problem arises.

Grant that Jesus Christ is true God and true man, and Redeemer of mankind—how do I enter into relation with Him? What has He, Who lived almost twenty centuries ago, to do with me? And what have I to do with Him? What possible reference could that Good Friday Cross have to my sins now? You probably often have seen planted on the rocks on the highways, signs reading: "Jesus Saves." You may have been very willing to admit this, but I am sure you must have added: "Certainly He saves, but how?"

CHAPTER SIX

Is Religion Purely Individual?

Have you ever heard anyone say: "I do not want any Church standing between me and God"? Do not be too harsh on them, for this statement is due to a misunderstanding. They would never say: "I do not want the United States Government standing between me and America." To say I want no one between God and me is anti-Christian because it implies that your brother is a barrier to God's grace and not a means to it.

Did not our Blessed Lord say that before offering your gift at the altar, you should first go and reconcile yourself with the brother whom you offended, and then come and offer your gift? Did He not also make love of God absolutely inseparable from love of neighbor? Did He not teach us to pray in the context of "Our Father", not "My Father"; "our daily bread", not "my daily bread"; "our trespasses" not "my trespasses"? And if God is a Father, then the others united to Him are our brothers, and, therefore, religion must be social.

You are not allowed individual interpretation of the Constitution of the United States. A Supreme Court does that for you. Why should you insist on individual interpretation of religion and begin all religious discussions with: "Now, this is what *I believe* about religion" or "*I feel* this way about God"?

Never were the sublime and beautiful realities put so much at the mercy of a stomach. Do you have your own individual astronomy and individual mathematics? Is not the personal pronoun "I" the most indecent of all the pronouns, and do you not dislike those people whose "I's" come too close together? Why then do you think the "I" used in isolation from your fellowmen is pleasing to God?

Say not, then, "religion is a private affair" any more than your birth is a private affair. You cannot be born alone; you cannot live alone; you cannot even die alone, for your death is tied up with property or at least with burial. You cannot practice religion alone any more than you can love alone.

What would happen to your patriotism if you said "Patriotism is an individual affair"? If you were the only citizen in America, could you be patriotic? If you were the only person in a town, could you be charitable? If, then, you cannot be kind alone or sacrificing alone or generous alone, how in the name of God do you expect to be religious alone? As generosity implies a neighbor, as patriotism implies fellow citizens, so religion implies fellowmen in relation to God.

All the best things of life come from solidarity and fellowship. God said to Hydrogen and Oxygen, say "Ours", and we have the oceans and tumbling cascades. The musician says to the scattered notes, say "Ours", and we have the symphony. The sun says to the planets, say "Ours", and we have a planetary system. Your mind says to ideas and words, say "Ours", and we have languages. America says to Americans, say "Ours", and we have democracy. Even the animals that say "Ours" survive in the struggle of existence: the bees, the ants, and the birds. But those dinosaurs and ichthyosaurs who roamed in isolation and made living a private affair have perished from the earth.

Now ask yourself the important question: How do I contact Christ the Redeemer? How does He save me? How do I come to know His Truth and His Will? How do I receive His Life? Do I contact Him as an individual by reading about Him and singing hymns to Him, or do I contact Him in fellowship and in community?

One way to answer that question is to inquire how mankind contacted God before the coming of Christ. Was religion a purely individual affair or was it corporate? Did God deal with individuals directly, or indirectly, that is, through a race or a community?

Search the Scriptures. You will find that God always dealt with mankind through human corporations or races, or moral bodies, presided over by a divinely chosen head. The Book of Genesis reveals that the history of mankind would be a warfare not between individuals, but between two seeds, two races, two corporate wholes: the power of darkness and the power of light. "I will put enmities between thee and the woman, and thy seed and her seed; she shall crush thy head, and thou shalt lie in wait for her heel" (Gen 3:15).

The head of the corporation of evil was Satan; the invisible head of the corporation of good was God, but God always chose a visible head of that community to act in His name. First, it was Noah, through whom with his kindred, salvation would come to *humanity*. Later, there came the new heads of this new spiritual corporation: Abraham, Isaac, and Jacob. To this community, God promised blessing and salvation. Later on, it was Moses whom God summoned as the head of His chosen people and through whom He promised their nation: "I will take you to myself for my people, I will be your God; and you shall know that I am the Lord your God, who brought you out from the work prison of the Egyptians" (Ex 6:7).

A covenant or contract was entered into between this community and God, in which God promised to bless them if they would obey His law and become His faithful witnesses and the bearers to the world of the Messiah, the "Expected of the Nations", the Savior of the World. After Moses, there are Joshua, David, and the prophets.

God always followed the same method. He never communicated His promises to individuals in the world at large, but to His chosen people through some chosen patriarch, or leader or king or prophet.

Whenever God willed to give new or special privileges to the community, He changed the name of its head, for example, Abraham, Jacob. This corporation, or chosen body, was not always faithful; it sometimes fell into idolatry, but despite their lapses, God was with them as His instrument, guiding, controlling, directing, so that whatever they did, His purpose never failed.

It was always the chosen community or moral body, and not the individual, which received God's revelation. Very likely, at the time of the flood, every individual might have liked to have his personal row boat, but God saved them in an ark under His own divinely appointed captain.

Throughout Jewish history, the community always holds first place, and the greatest punishment that could be inflicted upon any individual Jew was to be cut off from this corporate body. Even today to the Orthodox Jews, the most serious of all sanctions is in our modern language "to be put out of the synagogue", which it will be recalled was done to Spinoza.

So it came to pass that the most important word in the Old Testament was the word that expresses this corporation, or body, or congregation, or society. That word was קָהָל (*kāhāl*). About two hundred years before Christ, the Jews translated their Scriptures into Greek because so many Jews were living away from Israel in a Greek civilization. When the translators came to the Jewish word, *kāhál* (קָהָל), they translated it by the Greek word, *ecclesia*, which means "that which is called out", signifying that its members had been called out from the secular nations.

When finally the Messiah did come in the person of Christ Jesus, true God and true man, it was only natural to expect that God would now continue to deal with mankind in much the same way that He dealt with it before, namely, through a corporation presided over by a head whom He Himself would choose.

An "*ecclesia*" was already in existence when "God sent His Son, made of a woman, made under the law" (Gal 4:4). Our Lord was born in the very heart of a divinely chosen community or *ecclesia*. God, Who in previous times spoke through the prophets, now would speak through His Son to give the fullness of revelation.

Now that the fullness of time was come, God willed to elevate His *ecclesia* to the fullness of truth and power and grace. As once before He had named Abraham, Moses, and David as its head, so now He would name someone else as its head. Because new powers and privileges were to be given, He changed the name of that individual. As He changed Abram's name to Abraham, Jacob's name to Israel, so now He changed the name of the individual who is to be the new head, from Simon to Rock.

In English, his name is Peter. We lose the flavor of it in English because Peter and Rock are different words, but they are not in the language Our Lord spoke, nor in French, Greek, Latin, and several other languages. For example, in French Pierre means Rock and it also is the name of a man. In the original Greek, Our Lord said: "Thy name is Simon: Henceforth thou shalt be called the Rock."

On that day, when the Rock confessed that Christ was the Son of the Living God, the Divine Master answered: "Thou art Peter; and upon this rock I will build my church, and the gates of hell shall not prevail against it." From now on God's *ecclesia* would be built upon the Rock and it would be to the whole world God's chosen community for the communication of His Divine Life, as Israel before had been the community for the communication of its promise.

No wonder the Rock, in his first Sermon on Pentecost, spoke of the continuity of God's plan, namely, that "those things which God before had shewed by the mouth of all the prophets, that his Christ should suffer, he hath so fulfilled" (Acts 3:18) "by the hands of wicked men", but nonetheless in accordance with His "determinate counsel and foreknowledge" (Acts 2:23).

Our Lord said this new *ecclesia* would start small, like a mustard seed, but it would grow into a great tree, "so that the birds of the air may dwell under the shadow thereof" (Mk 4:32). It would be a new society with other ideals, purposes and goals than the world, and, hence, would be hated by the world as He was hated. Its members would be so closely united to each other and in Him, that if anyone did any kind act to any other member, for instance, give him food, or a drink of cold water, they would be doing it for Him. The unity between Him and it, He said, would be like the unity between the vine and its branches.

This new *ecclesia* or body was, therefore, not to be like a club that is formed by men coming together to a center for a common purpose. Rather, it was to be like a living body, from whose center life radiates until the organism is made perfect. It would not be men who would make a contribution to His organization; it would be He who would fill them with life.

If there was any human analogy for this *ecclesia*, it was the human body. As the body is composed of millions of tiny cells, each one living its own individual life, and yet no one able to live apart from the body, so this new *ecclesia* or Body would be made up of millions of individuals who were incorporated into Christ.

Just as one cell is not another, as an arm is not an ear, as an eye cannot say to the foot, "I can dispense with your services", so the teacher is not the priest, the missionary is generally not the family, and yet all through their different functions contribute to the order and beauty of the whole body, because it has one Invisible Head, Christ, and one visible head, the Rock, and one soul which is the Spirit of God.

The nucleus of this *ecclesia* or body was the Apostles, who were destined to spread out over the world, teaching all nations even to the consummation of the world.

To this new *ecclesia* or community, He promised to communicate His Truth, His Power, and His Redemption, which He had exercised through His physical body.

After all, was the Truth He taught to be limited to His time, and His generation? Was His Power to be confined to those who saw His Hands? Was His sanctification to be narrowed to those who climbed to Calvary? That men of His time might have no advantage over us, He gave to this new Body or *ecclesia*, His Truth, His Power, and His Sanctification. "I am the truth" (Jn 14:6), He said. But that truth He communicated to His *ecclesia*: "He that heareth you, heareth me; and he that despiseth you, despiseth me; and he that despiseth me, despiseth him that sent me" (Lk 10:16).

When, therefore, this new *ecclesia* began to teach, it would be He Who was teaching through them, just as He once taught through His human nature. Since it was God's truth, it would necessarily be infallible or free from error. If the Mind is Truth itself, then the tongue that speaks it is true or infallible.

The same was true of His Power. "And Jesus coming, spoke to them, saying: All power is given to me in heaven and in earth. Going therefore, teach ye all nations; baptizing them in the name of the Father, and of the Son, and of the Holy Ghost. Teaching them to observe all things whatsoever I have commanded you: and behold I am with you all days, even to the consummation of the world" (Mt 28:18–20). This Divine

Authority He communicated to the head of this His new *ecclesia* or body: "And whatsoever thou shalt bind upon earth, it shall be bound also in heaven: and whatsoever thou shalt loose on earth, it shall be loosed also in heaven" (Mt 16:19).

If you saw Christ lift His Hand, you would know that His Will commanded it. He was now saying that His Will, His Power, and His Authority would be exercised through another body, namely, His *ecclesia*. Disobedience to it, therefore, would be disobedience to Him, just as an insult to your body is an insult to your person.

Finally, He communicated His Sanctification and Priesthood to His new *ecclesia* or body. Would it not be a terrible thing if He did not? How would our sins be forgiven? Could Magdalen be forgiven and we be not forgiven? Somewhere this power to forgive sins is in the world today, and if He forgave her sins through a human nature, then, normally He will forgive our sins through other human natures in that *ecclesia* to whom He gave the power when He said: "Whose sins you shall forgive, they are forgiven them; and whose sins you shall retain, they are retained" (Jn 20:23).

These poor human natures who were given the power to forgive sins would not be holy as His nature was, but that would not spoil the absolution, for the human nature is only the instrument, not the cause of the forgiveness. The sunshine is not polluted because it shines through a dirty window.

The Apostles, we said, were the nucleus of this new *ecclesia* or body. Through them and their successors He would still continue to teach, to govern, and to sanctify. Up until the day of Pentecost, they were like chemicals in a laboratory. We know up to 100 percent of the chemicals which enter into the constitution of a human body, but we cannot make one, because we cannot create the vivifying, unifying principle, the soul.

In like manner, the Apostles had to wait until Christ sent the Holy Spirit of God to be their unifying soul, before they could become the Body of Christ or His *ecclesia*. Redemption could now go on. Just as He had taken a human nature from the womb of His Blessed Mother, overshadowed by the Holy Spirit, through which He exercised the office of Teacher, King, and Priest, so now He takes from the womb of humanity, overshadowed by the Pentecostal spirit, a new body, a new *ecclesia*, through which He still continues to teach, to govern, and to sanctify.

In the days of His earthly life, Christ's life and love and power were manifested under the limited and localized form of lips, hands, and feet; now, after His Resurrection and Ascension, they are manifested through other human natures, whom He has compacted and united to Himself as His New Body or *ecclesia*.

The Body of Christ is not only an organization; it is more like an organism. It no more stands between you and Christ than His physical body would have stood between you and His forgiveness. It was through His human body that He came to you on earth; it is through His Mystical Body or *Ecclesia* that He comes to you now.

Whenever, therefore, you confess your sins to a priest and hear the words: "I absolve you from your sins", you may rightly protest: "How can man forgive sins?" The answer is: "Man cannot forgive sins, but God can forgive sins *through man*." The Priest is not only the representative of God, He is also the representative of the *ecclesia*, the Community, through which God's pardon is communicated to man.

Also, God can speak infallibly through human nature. He can speak with Divine authority through man, as He can make a child an heir of Heaven through man. That is why God became man. If every contact you would have had with Our Lord Jesus Christ on earth would have been through His human nature, you may not expect now to have another contact with Him except through other human natures who represent His *ecclesia*.

Are you surprised to hear that Christ, Who is at the right hand of the Father with the glorified human nature, is now the Head of the new body of regenerated humanity, which has been growing since the day of Pentecost, and through which His Truth is still preached, His authority is still exercised, and His forgiveness still applied? Then, recall the story of the conversion of Paul, which took place a few years after the Ascension of our Lord.

This fiery Hebrew of the Hebrews grew up with an unholy hatred of Christ and things Christian, and as a young man he held the garments of those who stoned Stephen, the first Christian martyr. Paul was not just a bigot. He was a learned man, trained under Gamaliel, so powerful a disputant that the early Christians must often have wondered after the death of Stephen whom they could find to refute him.

In the Providence of God, it was reserved that Paul should refute a Paul. One day, he set out on a journey for Damascus, authorized by letters to seize the Christians of that city, bind them, and bring them back to Jerusalem. Breathing out hatred against the Lord, he departed to persecute the new infant *ecclesia*. Suddenly a great light shone about him and he fell to the ground, aroused by a voice like a bursting sea: "Saul, Saul, why persecutest thou me?" Nothingness dared to ask the name of Omnipotence: "Who art thou, Lord?" And He answered: "I am Jesus whom thou persecutest" (Acts 9:4, 5).

Saul was about to strike the body of believers in the city of Damascus, in exactly the same way as Christ's followers are persecuted in certain cities of the world today—and the Voice from Heaven says: "Saul, Saul, why persecutest thou me?"

Christ and His *Ecclesia* are the same. The risen Christ, only four or five years after He had left this earth, broke open the heavens to declare to Paul and the world, that in striking His Body you strike His Head, that the branches and the vine are one; that, when the Body of the Church is persecuted, it is Christ Who arises to speak. No wonder that the transformed and converted St. Paul understood Christ as well as the other apostles for he, too, had touched His Body.

Now we come to the answer of the question: How does Jesus save me? He saves me through His Body, or *ecclesia*, with this difference: His Body now is not physical, but mystical! It is made up of human natures infused with Divine Spirit. The only way in which we can be linked to another age is through a body of men, a body which, something in the manner of a natural body, renews itself through time.

The America of today is continuous with the America of Washington and Lincoln, through the body of government. Social clubs, baseball clubs, and steel corporations do not have the same membership now as ten decades ago, but they have maintained their continuity through generations through new members.

If you are over thirty years old, you remember two world wars. Suppose you were five hundred years old. You would then have known Shakespeare and Thomas More, Vincent de Paul and St. Teresa. Now suppose you were over nineteen hundred years old. Then you could say: I knew Christ. But you could not say that, could you, if you were only two hundred years old?

Now the body of Christ or the *ecclesia* which exists today is continuous with Him. It can say: "I was with

Christ when He taught; I heard Him; I was on Calvary; I saw Him rise from the dead; I was in the upper room on Pentecost. I was with Peter and Paul when they were martyred in Rome. I pre-existed the New Testament. I was already spread throughout the entire Roman Empire before a single Gospel was written and were it not for me, the Scripture would not exist today."

It can say: "I knew Augustine and Cyprian and Ambrose, Thomas and Bonaventure. I saw enemies come from without and enemies from within, but I have chanted a requiem over their graves, and I shall live all through time, not because I am a strong organization, for my members are weak, but because my soul, which is the Spirit of God, is immortal, and because my Invisible Head has promised that the gates of hell shall never prevail against me, until time shall be no more."

How do you establish contact with Christ? As the little children did, namely, by being taken into His Arms, by being incorporated to His Body. No wonder religion is confusing when you think of yourself in New York today, and Christ way back in Galilee over nineteen centuries ago. Where do you best know the spirit and the wisdom and the courage of a Lincoln? By visiting his Kentucky log cabin, or by living in America, which perpetuates and enshrines his memory?

Are you among those who think of the person of Christ as you do of Caesar, or Shakespeare; of Washington, or Lincoln? Does your religion think of Christ as one Who was here on this earth, and now is gone, and to Whom you can have relation only by following His example, or by reading His doctrine? Have you ever adverted to the fact that, if we could get no closer to our Divine Lord than by example and by doctrine, He hardly differs from any great figure of the past.

We can know Lincoln and Washington, too, by their teachings and their example. Grant that the example and teachings of Our Lord are incomparably superior, it, nevertheless, remains true, that if Christ cannot prolong Himself through space and time, then He differs but little from anyone who ever lived. If Christianity is only the memory of a great personage who taught, lived and suffered for an ideal in the past, and to whom we can get no closer than by our imagination flying back to Galilee, then Christianity is hardly worth preserving.

Since Christ is the true God as well as true man, He should be able to do what no man has ever been able to do, namely, to project His Life, His Truth and His Love to the very doors of our day and to the very threshold of our hearts. Then, those who lived in His times should have no advantages in love and forgiveness over those who live in our times. If He is not the Eternal Contemporary, He is not God.

No single drop of blood can exist apart from your body, but your body can exist without that single drop of blood, so the Body of Christ can live without you, but you cannot live without the Body of Christ. This is the meaning: "outside the *ecclesia* there is no salvation". All baptized souls, unless they guiltily refuse to, belong either in *reality* or in *intention* to this one *ecclesia* founded by Christ. Even unbaptized souls belong to it in *intention* if they live up to God's will according to the light of their conscience, and would accept Revelation if they knew about it.

You did not wait until you were twenty-one and then read the Constitution and American history. You were born out of the womb of America. As you were born out of the womb of political society, so as a Christian you were born out of the womb of Christ's society. You live by it, before you know it. It creates you spiritually by birth of the spirit, as your country created you by birth of the flesh.

The fact is the *ecclesia* is prior, both logically and chronologically, to its individual members. This *ecclesia* was spread throughout the entire Roman Empire before a single book of the New Testament was written. It was the Bible that grew out of the *ecclesia*, not the *ecclesia* out of the Bible.

If ever you have the happiness to visit the central church of all Christendom in Rome, I want you to lift your eyes above the tomb of that fisherman who was called Rock, to the greatest dome ever thrown against the vault of Heaven's blue, and read those words inscribed thereon: "Tu es Petrus et supra hanc petram, aedificabo *ecclesiam meam*": "Thou art the Rock"—that is the meaning of Peter—"And upon this rock I will build my church, and the gates of hell shall not prevail against it" (Mt 16:18). "And I will give to thee the keys of the kingdom of heaven. And whatsoever thou shalt bind upon earth, it shall be bound also in heaven: and whatsoever thou shalt loose on earth, it shall be loosed also in heaven" (Mt 16:19).

Ecclesia!—The very word the Jews used to describe Israel as God's community; the very word the Son of God Himself used at Caesarea-Philippi. And that *ecclesia* was built on Peter. Peter the Rock, who has lived through these nineteen hundred years and through 262 different personages, and whose name today is Pius XII [in 1946]. The word, *ecclesia*, means Church. The Catholic Church is the Mystical Body of Christ.

CHAPTER SEVEN

How You Are Remade

Have you ever thought that possibly there might be a higher life than the natural life you live now? I do not mean in the next world, but in this. Did you ever advert to the fact that you could know truths beyond the power of your reason and your experience; that you could have reserves of power for crisis, temptations, sorrow, and trial over and above those you now possess; that your soul could enjoy another life than the animal life you now live, and be possessed of a peace that the world cannot give?

The sinful woman, who came out at high noon to Jacob's well to draw water, was asked these questions by the One whom she later called "Savior". Did she know that there were waters for her soul as well as for her body? "If thou didst know the gift of God, and who he is that saith to thee, Give me to drink; thou perhaps wouldst have asked of him, and he would have given thee living water" (Jn 4:10).

You have no right to say there is no higher life than the physical life you now live, any more than the rose has a right to say there is no life above it. When God made a tree, He owed it to His own Truth, to give it all that was essential for its treeness and nothing more.

When God made you, He owed it to Himself to endow you with all that makes you a human being: a body and a soul endowed with reason and free will. He was not obliged to make you share His nature so that you would be His child and could call Him "Father", any more than He was obliged to make a rainbow that wrote poetry. If there is a higher life above the natural, you are no more entitled to it by right, than a crystal has a right to reason, or a cow has a right to sign title deeds, for these powers are beyond nature: they would be supernatural.

Because God created you, it does not follow that He exhausted all His love, any more than a mother exhausts all her love in giving birth to a child. In His Goodness, God could restore, if He willed it, all the privileges and gifts which were lost by our First Parents in the Fall.

Original sin, it has been said, is something like a severe illness which has upset our nature, with the result that there is a civil war going on inside us, our body rebelling against our soul, because our soul rebelled against God. Just as one country will sometimes "break off relations" with another country, so man by sin became separated from God and lost the gift by which he could attain his true supernatural end.

We have already learned that Christ by His Cross and Resurrection atoned for man's sins and broke down the barriers which separated us from Him. By bringing Divine Life into history, He made it possible for us in some way to receive it: "I am come that they may have life, and may have it more abundantly" (Jn 10:10).

If you thought about religion at all, you probably asked: But how can I contact that Divine Life of Christ? What have I to do with Christ who died over nineteen hundred years ago? Sing hymns? Listen to long sermons? Read the Scriptures? But these do not establish a vital relation with Him any more than singing hymns to Lincoln or reading his Gettysburg Address establishes personal relations with him.

Granted that Christ did pay your debts on Calvary when you were bankrupt from sin, how does that change your nature? You may ask: What is to prevent me, once my debts are paid, from being the same kind of creature I always was?

The answer is: You could be a new creature if Christ infused into your soul in some way His Divine Life! This would not have happened if Christ remained on earth in His human nature, for then He never would have been any closer to us than an embrace, or a spoken word, or a hand lifted in blessing. That is why He said: "It is expedient to you that I go: for if I go not, the Paraclete will not come to you; but if I go, I will send him to you" (Jn 16:7).

His departure on the Ascension was the very condition of the Apostles receiving Him intimately on Pentecost. If He sent His Spirit, then He would not be an external voice or an example to be copied, but a veritable life to be lived: "But when he, the Spirit of truth, is come, he will teach you all truth. For he shall not speak of himself; but what things soever he shall hear, he shall speak; and the things that are to come, he shall shew you" (Jn 16:13). "The Spirit of truth, whom the world cannot receive, because it seeth him not, nor knoweth him; but you shall know him; because he shall abide with you, and shall be in you" (Jn 14:17). "Lord, how is it, that thou wilt manifest thyself to us, and not to the world?" (Jn 14:22).

If the glorified Christ did send His Spirit into your souls, to restore you to His friendship, it would be purely gratuitous on His part, and being gratis, or a gift, it could appropriately be called "*grace*". "Every best gift, and every perfect gift, is from above, coming down from the Father of lights" (Jas 1:17).

If God did give this gift, He would have the same purpose you have in giving presents to your friends: to secure your happiness because He loves you. Of course, your gifts do not always make your friends happy, but God's gifts never fail to make us happy, because we cannot impart a new life, while God can. These supernatural gifts which the Holy Spirit, through the merits of Jesus Christ, pours into your soul, enable you to know more than you knew before, to love more than you loved before, and to do things which you could not do by your natural powers.

As a result of sin, your engine ran out of gasoline. God made you to run on His Divine fuel, and not even the best of human fuel will ignite in the combustion of love. By God's grace, however, you are made "partakers of the Divine Nature" so that something of God's life and activity is in you. In virtue of this, you grow up to be His Children, and God is your Father. Christ is your Brother, the Holy Spirit is the Guest in your soul, and Mary is your Mother, and you are made a sharer in that *ecclesia* through which you share in the Truth of Christ the Teacher, the Authority of Christ the King, and the sanctification of Christ the Priest.

Upon what conditions can I receive this gift of a higher life? What are the normal ways in which this Divine Life is given? What effect will it have on me? How can you contact this Divine Life that Christ merited for you?

In somewhat the same way that everything in nature receives a higher life than that which it naturally possesses: (a) by something higher coming down to that which is lower and (b) by the lower surrendering its imperfect nature in order to be incorporated into something higher.

How can the moisture, the carbons, and the phosphates in the earth ever live in the plant? First, the plant life must descend to them, take them up into its roots and branches, while the chemicals themselves must abandon the crude lifeless state they have in nature. If the plant could speak, it would say to the chemicals: "Unless you die to yourselves, you cannot live in my kingdom." Actually, the sunshine, chemicals, and moisture now begin to thrill with life and vitality in the plant.

If the animal could speak, it would say to the plants: "Unless you die to your lower life of mere vegetation and submit yourself momentarily to the jaws of death, you cannot live in my kingdom. Once you live in me, you will share a life that not merely vegetates, but feels and moves and tastes and sees." Man in his turn, going down to that which is lower, says to the animals: "Unless you die to yourself by submitting to the sacrificial death, you cannot live in my kingdom. But if you die to yourself, you shall share a life that is not merely sensible, but one that thinks and loves, has ideals, laughs, and is artistic."

This is precisely what Christ says to you: "Unless you die to yourself, you cannot live in My Kingdom"—but with this difference: since we are persons, which chemicals, plants, and animals are not, the sacrifice enjoined on us is not physical, but spiritual. We do not have our personality destroyed, as a plant's nature is destroyed when taken into the beast.

Otherwise the law holds good. The higher comes down to the lower; the Divine descends into the human.

Such was the Incarnation: God came down to man. On the other hand, man must die to his sinful nature, his old Adam, his heritage of the Fall, and this he can do only by sacrifice and by taking up "his cross daily" and following Him. "Unless the grain of wheat falling into the ground die, itself remaineth alone. But if it die, it bringeth forth much fruit. He that loveth his life shall lose it; and he that hateth his life in this world, keepeth it unto life eternal" (Jn 12:24, 25).

The law of transformation holds sway; chemicals are lifted into plants, plants into animals, animals into man, and since man is free, he can freely will, through the Graciousness of God, to be lifted up into Christ, so that he can say: "And I live, now not I; but Christ liveth in me" (Gal 2:20). God came down to the level of man that He might in some way lift man to the level of God.

To be a Christian is to be born of Christ, so that our poor, weak, sinful human nature is not gilded over as so much brass, but rather is re-created, so that we become a "new creature". Our human nature inherited from Adam does not become better; it dies and is reborn as Christ died on Calvary and rose from the dead.

Even with this infusion of Divine life you must still use your will. After your car is filled with gasoline, it will not drive itself. Grace does not work like a penny in a slot machine. Grace will move you only when you want it to move you, and only when you let it move you. The supernatural order supposes the freedom of the natural order, but it does not destroy it. An alarm clock will awaken you in the morning but it will not make you get up. God's grace will aid, direct, and perfect your human actions, but only on condition that you freely cooperate with it. God breaks down no doors.

Becoming a Christian is, therefore, a regeneration, the living of a new life above the human. The life of the body is the soul; the life of the soul is Christ. Because grace or supernatural life is a regeneration, it makes no difference what your background is, or how wicked you were, or how many sins you committed.

Once by an act of will you make God's life your own, you live by a new Spirit, are governed by new laws, breathe a different atmosphere, and have an entirely new set of values. You are not merely made solvent after having become bankrupt by sin; you are made a new man: a new man in Christ.

Never believe those who say: "Once a thief, always a thief". Or, "You are wasting your money on that worthless creature." The Christian claim is that you are not! You can put off your old nature and put on a new. Since grace is regeneration, it makes little difference what your old nature was.

If I throw away an old coat, it makes little difference if I do so because it is torn, or because it is spotted with soup, or because it is moth-eaten, or because it is faded. The only thing that matters is: I throw it away. And when I throw it away, I get a new coat. The difference is that, by being reborn in Christ, you do not throw away something external; you bury your nature with Christ. You do it because you get a new nature, one that partakes of the very nature of God. In the strong language of St. John, "We are born of God" (Jn 1:13).

Though you are regenerated to share the Christ life, you are not dispensed from the necessity of preserving that life against evil, as you preserve your physical life by resistance to disease and death. Earth is not Heaven, and not all the gifts we lost by original sin will be restored to us until the Final Resurrection.

What the grace of God does is to set you on the right road. Up to this time, you were on the wrong road; you were fighting against brambles, brushing thorns aside, stumbling over rocks, simply never getting anywhere. When you become a Christian, Our Divine Lord sets you on the right track. The road is marked with signs or dogmas: telling you the way to go and which detours to avoid.

Never think that when the Church tells you, "Avoid this path—Poison Ivy", that is restricting your freedom. The Church gives you a map and marks your destination. Though you are on the right road, you still retain some of the effects of having been on the wrong road. You are still hungry, your clothes are torn, and your feet are tired.

Even on the right road, you will still have to walk and pick out a few thorns, but it will not be too difficult, for all along that road you will find places to eat the Bread of Life, first-aid stations where your thorns can be picked out, and above all you will find divinely appointed guides whose sole business it is to bring you safely to the City of Peace.

While some people are alive in body, they may be dead in soul. When they die, they undergo what Scripture calls the "double death"; they are dead now to both the life of the body and the life of the soul. That makes clear what St. John said: "You call yourselves living and yet you are dead."

In God's eyes, there are perhaps more spiritual corpses walking around the streets today in apparent life, than there are physical corpses being carried to the graves. They can breathe, eat, think, but they are dead to the truth above reason, to love beyond the grave. Only God's grace can be to them the Resurrection and the Life.

What are the normal ways in which this Divine Life of Christ is given, if I want to receive it?

This question breaks down the time and space interval that separates us from Calvary. It asks: How is Christ's forgiveness available to me right now? How could I, if I wanted to, make my marriage a supernatural rather than a natural one? How could I develop spiritually in Christ as I develop physically? How can I contact the Divine Life?

All these questions have been answered by our Blessed Lord. Knowing that you had a body as well as a soul, He chose not to communicate His Divine Life to you invisibly. If you were an angel, you would need no sensible evidence that His Life was being poured into your soul. Being physical as well as spiritual, He willed normally to give you His supernatural life or grace under the symbol of some material sign.

Since your natural life is already full of material things that are symbols or channels for the invisible, He chose to fill your supernatural life with such external signs. For example, a handshake is more than the clasping of hands; it is the channel for the communication of something invisible and deep in the soul, namely, friendship. In other words, it is a sacrament, an outward sign of an inward reality. A letter or a spoken word is a sacrament in the broad sense of the term for it communicates more than that which meets the eye or the ear.

Our Divine Lord, not only in tribute to our physical nature, but also in order to bring the materials of a chaotic world again in the Divine order, instituted Sacraments. A Sacrament is a material sign or symbol through which God communicates His Divine Life. Through them He pours into your souls *now* the very Life He purchases for you on Calvary.

Since the material universe fell through man's sin, why should not the material universe by Christ's redemption minister unto justification?

Why should not the Divine Pharmacist who made minerals, roots, vegetables to minister to the physical

life of man, also make use of wheat and oil and water as
the medicine of His supernatural life? You would then
know your sins were being washed away through the
visible sign, water. You would know that your spiritual
life was being nourished by the external sign of that reality, namely, bread.

Was it not Goethe who said: "The highest cannot
be spoken; it can only be acted"? The Sacraments are the
drama of God. He conceived them; He acts them; He
elevates through them. Their efficacy does not depend on
our subjective belief; they give Divine Life by the mere
fact that we receive them. If we enter into them worthily,
we will find ourselves lifted up into the supernatural life
and perfected in it. If we enter into these Divine realities
lightly, this does not mean that nothing happens.

A grain of radium might be taken by one ill with
cancer, as the promise of his future health. If, however,
it is handled carelessly, it may cause, not restoration of
health, but instead the most frightful and death-dealing
burns. In like manner, the very thing that should minister to eternal salvation could, by unworthiness, minister
unto eternal damnation.

How many Sacraments are there? Or how many
ways has God chosen to communicate His Divine Life?
There are seven, and there can be only seven for there
are seven conditions of all life either physical or spiritual.
Five of these refer to the individual life of man, and two
to his social life.

To live in individual physical life, five conditions must be fulfilled:

1. You must be born.
2. You must be nourished.
3. You must grow to maturity.
4. You must heal your wounds.
5. You must drive out traces of disease, for a disease is different from a wound.

Then, as a social being, two more conditions are necessary.

1. You must propagate the human species.
2. You must live under government.

You simply cannot think of physical life continuing except on these conditions.

Since there is another life above the natural, namely, the supernatural, it follows that there are seven conditions necessary for living the life of the new creature in Christ.

1. You cannot live a natural life unless you are born to it; neither can you live the Christ-life unless you are born to it. That is the Sacrament of Baptism, by which we die to the old nature and are born to the new. As original sin is washed away, you are incorporated into the fellowship of the Kingdom of God.

2. As you cannot live a natural life unless you nourish yourself, so you cannot lead a supernatural life unless you nourish yourself. This is the Holy Eucharist in which you receive the Bread of Life by which you are not only united to Christ, but to all who eat of that Bread in the fellowship of the Body of Christ.

3. As you cannot lead a perfect natural life unless you grow to maturity and assume responsibilities of your state in life, so you cannot lead a perfect supernatural life unless you grow into the full responsibilities of the Christian life. This is the Sacrament of Confirmation, wherein you fulfill your tasks as a soldier and apostle within the Mystical Body of Christ, through the infusion of a spirit of wisdom and counsel and other gifts which enable you to defend and understand and diffuse the Spirit of Christ.

4. When you wound your natural life, you must be healed; when you wound your supernatural life by sin, you must be absolved. That is the Sacrament of Penance.

5. If your natural life suffers from a disease, the traces of that disease must be banished. Since no disease ever leaves traces comparable to the disease of sin in the supernatural life, it follows that, before meeting your God, the remains of sin must be blotted out. That is the Sacrament of Extreme Unction [the Anointing of the Sick], which restores the harmony of organization

between soul and body, that it may fulfill its vocation in time or in eternity.

You are not mere individuals in religion. You are members of the Body of Christ. In order that this spiritual corporation may perfect itself, and grow, two more conditions must be fulfilled.

6. As the natural life is perfected by propagation of the human species, so the supernatural life of the Kingdom of God is perfected by raising children of God. That is the Sacrament of Matrimony, by which husband and wife are made two in one flesh to symbolize the union of Christ and His Church: unbreakable, true, and loving.

7. Finally, as your natural life must be lived under law and government, so your supernatural life must be lived under spiritual government, and this is the Sacrament of Holy Orders by which Christ's priesthood is prolonged to apply the fruits of law and order to all the members of His Mystical Body.

Calvary is a great and tremendous reservoir of merit. From it flow seven channels to the human soul, and through those channels passes the same Divine Life that fills the reservoir, the only difference being the measure of the life received. While Christ is the Natural Son of God, we are only adopted sons. Two of these channels can flow into souls in the state of sin: Baptism and Penance, to beget or renew Divine Life, for both cleanse us from death: the death of original sin and the death of personal sin. All the others flow usually to a soul already vivified by the Divine Life.

Judge not the existence of those Divine outpourings by the matter you see in the Sacraments, which are but the signs of the life within; judge not baptism by the water, or the Eucharist by its Bread any more than you judge the joy of friendship by a handshake or an embrace. What is the spoken word but the air put in movement? But when the soul is in it, it becomes eloquence, justice, truth, courage to do and die.

Think of what a word is when God puts His Spirit in it! What is water but a union of hydrogen and oxygen? Put the genius of man into it and it becomes vapor, commerce, power, civilization. Think of what water is when God puts Himself into it. What is bread but the mere chemical combinations of wheat, water, and yeast? Unite it with the soul of man and it becomes strength, life, food, joy. Think of what bread is when God changes it into Himself.

Likewise, for the other Sacraments: that which strikes the eye in them is weak and poor, but that which strikes the soul in them is Divine. They, too, like the men who receive them, are material and spiritual, and like the Christ who instituted them, are made up of the visible and the Divine. Thanks to them, the words of

Our Lord are fulfilled: "I am come that they may have life, and may have it more abundantly."

In all the shocks of life, He meets us with His Life and the Redemption of His Cross—at the cradle when we are born, at the moment of our death; when we are at peace, and when we are in sin; when we share our life socially, and when we share it religiously; and in each and every instance He has used visible signs that we may know when we receive an inrush of the Life of God.

The procession of life is not upward from the beast to man, but downward from God to man. The source of Divine Life whence the great procession starts is in God: Father, Son, and Holy Ghost. From out of that Immensity the Procession of Life moved as the Father sent His Divine Son into the world of broken hearts.

Assuming a human nature from the Blessed Mother, the Procession of Divine Life moved on the earth in the Person of Jesus Christ, and finally it wound its way up the hill of Calvary, and on Good Friday a soldier struck a lance into the side of that Sacred Humanity—blood and water poured forth: blood the price of our Redemption, and water the symbol of our regeneration. The Son sent by His Father now returns to the Father, and from the Eternal Godhead the Procession of Life moves on as the Father and the Son send their Holy Spirit full of Truth and Love to the Mystical Body on the day of Pentecost.

Striking that Mystical Body as the brightness of the sun striking a prism splits up into the seven rays of the spectrum, the Procession of Divine Life broke up into the Seven Sacraments, to flood the members of that Body with Divine Life for the seven states from the cradle to the grave.

For nineteen hundred years, Life has flowed from the Head in Heaven to the Body on earth, without increase or decrease, for as Creation added nothing to the Being of God, so the Church added nothing to the Life of God.

The Procession of Life moves on as Christ once more walks the earth in His Mystical Body. The River Jordan flows into every baptismal font as Christ baptizes a soul into that Body of which He is the Head; the Pentecost fires blaze again at every Confirmation as Christ sends His Spirit to make us valiant soldiers of His Body on earth.

The Cenacle table is moved to our Communion rails as Christ once more gives the Bread of Life that the members of His Body may be one as He and the Father are one. Simon's house is become a Confessional box as Christ once more raises His hands to penitent sinners bidding them go in peace and sin no more.

The cross at the right of Calvary's central Cross becomes the symbol of a million deathbeds as Christ once more purifies the soul for its last journey into Paradise, even on the very day of death. Cana's nuptials are repeated at the foot of every altar as Christ once more blesses the love that unites man and wife in an unbreakable bond, as the Holy Spirit has united Him and His Spouse, the Church, in a union of bliss through the endless eternity. The Last Supper is revivified at every ordination ceremony as Christ once more says to those whom He has chosen out of the world, "Do this for a commemoration of Me" (Lk 22:19).

Finally, when the great Procession of Life has wound its way through all nations and all peoples, infusing them with the Divine Life unto the fullness and perfection of His Mystical Body; when Christ shall have grown to His full stature, then will the Procession turn back once more to its Source in Heaven, where all nature will be subject to man as in the sacramental principle, where man will be subject to Christ as in the Incarnation, where Christ in His human nature will be subject to the Father, and where God shall be all in all.

What then, are some of the effects of this Divine Life in your soul?

The first is the Divine Presence: God begins to dwell in your soul: "If any one loves me, he will keep my word, and my Father will love him, and we will come to him, and will make our abode with him" (Jn 14:23). "God is charity: and he that abideth in charity, abideth in God, and God in him" (1 Jn 4:16).

Like Adam in the Garden, you walk in the company of God. God is nearer to you, if your soul is in the state of grace, than the air you breathe and the friends you see. This presence is not psychological, that is, you do not achieve it by imagining yourself in His Presence; neither is it a presence through a keen memory of the scenes of Our Lord's life; it is obviously not a material presence as salt is in a box for we are in the realm of spirit. It is not the same as the universal presence of God in the world by His creative act for otherwise there would be no difference between a soul in the state of grace and a soul in the state of sin.

While God is everywhere by His Creative Power, He is not everywhere by the in-dwelling of His grace. A carpenter is in the bench he made by his power, his idea, and his purpose, but the carpenter is in his son in a much more special way. In like manner, by grace, God dwells in your soul more intimately than He is by creation.

God is present by creation in the stars, and the flowers, and the sunset, without any answering presence on their part; there is no consciousness of His Presence. By grace, however, God becomes present in you a new way; He is now not only present to you by power, He is *in* you by *love*. "Try your own selves if you be in the faith; prove ye yourselves. Know you not your own selves, that Christ Jesus is in you, unless perhaps you be reprobates?" (2 Cor 13:5).

He is present more intimately than the truth of the multiplication table is in your mind, or the love of your mother is in your will. A new conscious relationship is established, not that of Creator and creature, but of Spouse and spouse—Bridegroom and bride. Your soul now looks on God not just as a Being Who made you and to Whom you are bound by justice, but as a Love Who redeemed you and to Whom you are united by reciprocal acts of love.

It is only when you can freely use a thing and enjoy it, that you can be said to possess it. By grace, God is in your soul. Your soul is then not a passive recipient of God's Power and Love and Truth, as a marble receives a sculptor's chisel. It may even react habitually by holding Him and possessing Him permanently.

In this you have the answer to the question: What does it mean to be a Christian? Christianity is not a system of ethics; it is a life. It is not good advice; it is Divine adoption. Being a Christian does not consist in being kind to the poor, going to Church, reading the Bible, singing hymns, being generous to relief agencies, just to employees, gentle to cripples, serving on Church committees, though it includes all of these. It is first and foremost a *love relationship*.

As you can never become a member of a family by doing generous deeds, but only by being born into it out of love, so you can never become a Christian by doing good things, but only by being born to it through Divine Love. *Doing* good things to a man does not make you his son, but *being* a son does make you do good things.

Christianity begins with *being*, not with doing, with life and not with action. If you have the life of a plant, you will bloom like a plant; if you have the life of a monkey, you will act like a monkey. If you have the life of a man, you will do the things a man does, but if you have the Life of Christ in you, you will act like a Christian. You are like your parents because you partake of their nature; you are like God if you partake of His Nature. What a man does is the externalization of what he *is*.

Most people have their actions governed by their background, for example, you think a certain way in order to defend your class or your wealth or your want of it; you even build up a philosophy to suit the way you live; you do certain things because they are profitable or pleasant to you; you hate certain people because they are a reproach to your conscience or because they challenge your egotism. Your psycho-physical disposition is the center of your life and, therefore, of your actions. You are, in a word, self-determined.

To be a Christian means to discard self as the supreme determinant of actions; it means to put on the mind of Christ so as to be governed by Christ's truths; to surrender your will to His Will, and to do all things that are pleasing to Him, not to you; to control your emotional attitudes. In other words, your life instead of being self-determined is Christ-determined.

As a result of this Divine in-dwelling these consequences follow:

Your body by grace becomes a Temple of God. A temple is a place where God dwells and since God dwells

in your soul by grace, your body is His Temple: "Know
you not that you are the temple of God, and that the
Spirit of God dwelleth in you?" (1 Cor 3:16). This is
the basic reason why you as a Christian must be pure in
thought and deed, not that you must avoid diseases and
be hygienic but because, conscious that your body is the
Temple of God, you will never pollute it by sin. You
will, therefore, never have it cremated after death.[1] A
dead body, whose soul died in the state of grace, is like
a church closed for repairs. Your soul will be reunited
to your body after the Resurrection. As it shocks you to
see a church bombed, it shocks the Church to see a
body cremated.

The fact that God dwells in your soul is the founda-
tion of what is called your *interior* life. Many baptized
souls are ignorant of this mystery and remain un-
aware of it for the most part of their lives, their religion
being only a memory of Jesus on earth, or else a God
seated on a throne way up in the heavens. One day
Louise de France, the daughter of Louis XV, said to
her governess in a fit of temper: "Know you not that I
am the daughter of your king?" to which the governess
answered: "And know you not that I am the daughter
of your God".

[1] At the time that then-Monsignor Sheen was writing, cremation was not allowed.
This discipline later changed: "The Church permits cremation, provided that it
does not demonstrate a denial of faith in the resurrection of the body (Cf. Code
of Canon Law, canon 1176, section 3)" (*Catechism of the Catholic Church*, 2nd ed.,
no. 2301 [Vatican City: Libreria Editrice Vaticana, 1997])—ED.

One of the reasons we seldom advert to the Divine Presence in our souls by grace is because we are too absorbed by creatures. That is why the Christian life is called warfare, why it demands mortification. As physical life is the sum of forces which resist death, so the spiritual life is, in a way, the sum of the forces which resist sin.

By virtue of God's grace, you become an adopted son of God and cease to be just a mere creature. Adoption means the reception of a stranger into a family. A person will adopt a child because he lacks one. God never does that for God already has a Son which exhausts the fullness of perfection.

Furthermore, though an adopted child on earth can be given the name, the title, the wealth, and the influence of him who adopted, yet the adopted one could never receive his life. But God can make you share His Life. Just as your beauty, your strength, your learning, your honesty, make you pleasing to your friends, so God by the infusion of His good makes us share in His Nature, His Goodness, His Truth, and His Beauty and, therefore, makes us pleasing to Him.

Thus, you become, through Our Lord's merits, that which Adam lost by sin: God's own child. "By this is the spirit of God known. Every spirit which confesseth that Jesus Christ is come in the flesh, is of God" (1 Jn 4:2).

In virtue of sharing your sonship, Heaven becomes not a privilege, but a right. "And if sons, heirs also"

(Rom 8:17). God the Father then will cease to be to you a gray-bearded potentate who dwells far off in the heavens, but in the truest sense One Whom you now can approach as a child, a son crying, "Father." And if you ever fell into sin like the Prodigal Son, you could say: "I will arise and go to the Father."

If you are the adopted son of the Heavenly Father, then you are also a brother of Christ, and all other sons of the Father are also His brethren. What you do to them, you will do to Him. Every time you give a drink of water to a fellowman, or bind his wounds, or wipe away his tears, or clothe his impoverished body, or feed his body, you are doing it to Christ. "As long as you did it to one of these my least brethren, you did it to me" (Mt 25:40).

Because you are a son of the Heavenly Father, and a brother of Christ, you also have Christ's Mother as your Mother. More than that, you are made partaker of the divine nature and, as such, of the Holy Spirit of God. As the Holy Spirit is the eternal bond, which unites the Father and Son, so the Holy Spirit now becomes the bond uniting you both to God and to all the other members of the *ecclesia* of God. The Holy Spirit of God thus becomes the source of your inspiration and guidance.

In moments of crisis and doubt, in worries whether to undertake this task or omit it, to go on this journey or not, listen to the voice of the Spirit within. The union of your soul and the Holy Spirit can become a kind of spiritual marriage, giving the joys of the spirit born of a unity that leaves all other joys as sorrows, and all other beauty as pain. For the first time in your life, you would begin to love, not that which is lovely, but that which is Love: The Spirit of the Most High God.

Be conscious that your every word, thought, and deed are enacted before a Divine Audience. As you would not break the speed laws if a policeman were around, so you will not break the Divine Laws, but not because you fear God, rather, because you love Him.

Let the Christ be the Unseen Guest at your every meal; your Divine Host in every visit; your Captain in every war; your Fellow Worker in every task; your Father in every home; your Giver of every gift; the Listener in your conversation; your Companion in every walk; your Visitor at every knock, and your Neighbor in every street; your Owner of every treasure and your Lover in every love.

When you fail to measure up to your Christian privilege, be not discouraged, for discouragement is a form of pride. The reason you are sad is because you looked to yourself and not to God; to your failing, not to His Love. You will shake off your faults more readily when you love God than when you criticize yourselves. The sick person looks happily at the physician, not at his wounds. You have always the right to love Him in your heart, even though now and then you do not love Him in your acts. Keep no accounts with God or you will always be so hopelessly in debt as to be bankrupt.

Do not fear God for perfect love casteth out fear. God is biased in your favor. Would you rather be judged by the Justice of the Peace of your town on the last day; or by the King of Peace? Most certainly by God, would you not? David even chose a punishment at God's hands rather than man's for God he knew would be more lenient.

God is more lenient than you because He is perfectly good and, therefore, loves you more. Be bold enough, then, to believe that God is on your side, even when you forget to be on His. Live your life, then, not by law, but by love. As St. Augustine put it: "Love God and then do whatever you please." If you love God, you will never do anything to hurt Him, and, therefore, never make yourself unhappy.

CHAPTER EIGHT

Judgment

If there is anything that characterizes your life, it is an intolerance of boundaries. You want the infinite. That is why you are so often disappointed: you see a tremendous disproportion between the ideal you conceived, and the reality which you attained. Still, you go on searching, simply because you have an indefinite capacity for *more*. You simply cannot imagine yourself as undesirous of *more*.

Nature sets certain limits to *more* for your bodies. A boy's eyes are bigger than his stomach. There is a limit to bodily pleasures. They reach a point where they become a pain, as we become sickened of their own "too much". But there are no limits to the desires of your soul. They never reach a point of satiety. There are no limits to the truth you can know, to the life you can live, and to the love you can enjoy, and to the beauty you can experience.

If this life were all, think of how much your soul would be cheated. You would be as frustrated as a woman mad about fashions, who was put into a room where there were a thousand hats but not a single mirror.

Since you have a body and a soul, you can make either one the master; you can make the body serve the soul which is the Christian way, or you can make the soul serve the body which is the miserable way. It is that choice which makes life so serious.

There would be no fun in playing games unless there were a chance to lose. There would be no zest in battle if crowns of merit rested suspended over those who do not fight. There would be no interest in drama if the characters were puppets. And there would be no point to life unless there were great and eternal destinies at stake, in which we may say Aye or Nay to our eternal salvation. "And fear ye not them that kill the body, and are not able to kill the soul: but rather fear him that can destroy both soul and body in hell" (Mt 10:28). "For what doth it profit a man, if he gain the whole world, and suffer the loss of his own soul? Or what exchange shall a man give for his soul?" (Mt 16:26).

There will eventually come a moment in your life when this trial will be over. I know it is a subject about which modern minds do not like to hear. The fact of death is so disguised today that morticians would, if they could, make us believe there is happiness in every box. The modern mind feels awkward in the face of death. He does not know how to extend sympathy; he scruples not at reading detective stories in which there are a dozen deaths, but that is because he concentrates on the circumstances preceding death rather than on the eternal issues involved in death. He never asks: "Saved or lost?", but only: "Who killed Cock Robin?"

St. Paul tells us, not in a harsh, stoic manner, that if we are to live to Christ, we must "die daily". A happy death is a masterpiece and no masterpiece was ever perfected in a day. Dubois spent seven years in making the wax model for his celebrated statue of Joan of Arc. One day the model was finished and the bronze was poured into it. The statue stands today as a ravishing perfection of the sculptor's art. In like manner, our death at the end of our natural existence must appear as a ravishing perfection of the many years of labor we have given over to its mold by dying daily.

The greatest reason why we fear death is because we have never prepared for it. Most of us die only once when we should have died a thousand times—aye, when we should have died daily. Death is a terrible thing for him who dies only when he dies; but it is a beautiful thing for him who dies before he dies.

There is an interesting inscription over the tomb of Duns Scotus in Cologne which reads: "Semel sepultus bis mortuus": a double death preceded his burial. There is not one traveler in a hundred who understands the mystery of love behind it.

After death there is no remedy for an evil life. But before death there is a remedy: it is by dying to ourselves, in which we follow that law of immolation which is the law of the whole universe. There is no other way of entering into a higher life except by dying to the lower; there is no possibility of man's enjoying an ennobled existence in Christ unless he is torn up from the old Adam. To him who leads a mortified life in Christ, death then never comes like a thief in the night because it is he who takes it by surprise. We die daily in order to try dying and then again in order to succeed.

Whether we like it or not, there is no escaping the truth: "It is appointed unto men once to die, and after this the judgment" (Heb 9:27). As your relatives and friends gather around you to ask: "How much did he leave?" the angels will ask, "How much did he take with him?"

Judgment will be twofold. You will be judged at the moment of your death, which is the particular judgment, and you will be judged on the last day of the world, which is the general judgment. The first judgment is because you are a person and are, therefore, individually responsible for your free acts; your work will follow you. The second Judgment will be because you worked out your salvation in the context of a social order, and the Mystical Body of Christ; therefore you must be judged by your repercussions upon it.

What will the judgment be like, and here we refer to the particular judgment? It will be an evaluation of yourself as you really are. In each of us there are several persons: there is the person others think you are; there is the person *you* think you are; there is the person you *really are.*

During life it is easy for us to believe our own press notices, and to believe our publicity, to take ourselves very seriously, to judge ourselves by public opinion rather than by eternal truth, hence we may and do think ourselves good because our neighbor is so wicked. We may even judge our virtues by the vices from which we abstain. If we made our money under capitalists, we think labor organizations are wicked; if we made it organizing labor unions, we think capitalism is evil; if we come from the city, we look down on people from the country; we think because a person speaks with an accent, he is unimportant, that if he is black, or brown, or yellow, he is of less value.

Our very enthusiasm for the common man may be because we hate the rich; our political affiliations affect our moral judgment and make us support the party right or wrong. St. Paul describes it as going through life wearing smoked glasses: "We see now through a glass in a dark manner; but then face to face. Now I know in part; but then I shall know even as I am known" (1 Cor 13:12).

When the split second of judgment comes, you will take off these smoked glasses and see yourself as you really are. Now what are you *really*? You are what you are, not by your emotions, your feelings, your likes and dislikes, but by your *choices*. The decisions of your free will will be the content of your judgment.

To change the figure: We are all on the roadway of life in this world, but we travel in different vehicles: some in trucks, some in jeeps, some in ambulances, others in twelve-cylinder cars, others in flivvers, and others in trucks. But each of us does the driving.

The judgment at death is something like being stopped by a motor cop, except, thank heaven, the Good Lord is not as hard as the motor cops. When we are stopped, God does not say: "What kind of a car did you drive?" He is no respecter of persons. He asks: "How well did you drive? Did you obey the laws?"

At death we leave behind our vehicles, that is, our emotions, prejudices, feelings, our state in life, our opportunities, the accidents of talent, beauty, intelligence, and position. Hence, it will make no difference to God if we were crippled, over-ignorant, or hated by the world. Our judgment will be based not on our background or social position, but on the way we lived, the choices we made, and whether we obeyed the law!

Think not, then, that at the moment of judgment you will argue a case. You will plead no extenuating circumstances; you will not ask for a change of venue, nor for a new jury, nor allege an unfair trial. You will be your own judge. You will be your own jury; you will pass your own sentence. God will merely seal your judgment.

What is judgment? From God's point of view, judgment is a recognition. Two souls appear before the sight of God in that split second after death. One is in the state of grace, the other is not. The Judge looks into the soul in the state of grace. He sees there a resemblance of His nature, for grace is the participation in Divine Nature.

Just as a mother knows her child because of the resemblance of nature, so, too, God knows His own children by resemblance of nature. If we are born of Him, He knows it. Seeing in that soul His likeness, the Sovereign Judge, Our Lord and Savior Jesus Christ, says unto it: "Come, ye blessed of My Father. I have taught you to pray, 'Our Father'. I am the natural Son; you, the adopted son. Come into the Kingdom I have prepared for you from all eternity."

The other soul, not possessing the family traits and likeness of the Trinity, meets an entirely different reception from the Judge. As a mother knows that her neighbor's son is not her own, because there is no participation in her nature, so too, Jesus Christ, seeing in the sinful soul no participation of His nature, can only say those words which signify non-recognition, "I know you not", and it is a terrible thing not to be known by God!

Such is judgment from the Divine point of view. From the human point of view, it is also a recognition, but a recognition of unfitness or fitness. A very distinguished visitor is announced at the door, but I am in my working clothes, my hands and face are dirty. I am in no condition to present myself before such an august personage, and I refuse to see him until I can improve my appearance.

A soul stained with sin acts very much the same when it goes before the judgment seat of God. It sees on one hand His Majesty, His Purity, His Brilliance, and on the other its own baseness, its sinfulness, its unworthiness. It does not entreat nor argue, it does not plead a case—it sees; and from out of the depths comes its own judgment, "Oh, Lord, I am not worthy."

The soul that is stained with venial sins casts itself into Purgatory to wash its baptismal robes, but the soul irremediably stained—the soul dead to Divine Life—casts itself into hell just as naturally as a stone which is released from my hand falls to the ground.

Three possible destinies await you at death:

Hell: Pain without Love
Purgatory: Pain with Love
Heaven: Love without Pain.

CHAPTER NINE

Purgatory

There is one word which to modern ears probably signifies the unreal, the fictional, and even the absurd in the Christian vision of life, and that is the word, "Purgatory". Although the Christian world believed in it for sixteen centuries, for the last three hundred years it has ceased to be a belief outside the Church, and has been regarded as a mere product of the imagination, rather than as the fruit of sound reason and inspiration.

It is quite true to say that the belief in Purgatory has declined in just the proportion that the modern mind forgot the two most important things in the world: the Purity of God and the heinousness of sin. Once both these vital beliefs are admitted, the doctrine of Purgatory is unescapable.

What is Purgatory but a place or condition of temporal punishment for those who depart this life in God's grace, but are not entirely free from venial faults or have not entirely paid the satisfaction due to their transgressions? Purgatory is that place in which the Love of God tempers the Justice of God, and, secondly, where the love of man tempers the injustice of man.

First, Purgatory is where the Love of God tempers the Justice of God. The necessity of Purgatory is grounded upon the absolute purity of God. In the Book of Revelation we read of the great beauty of His city, of the pure gold, with its walls of jasper and its spotless light, which is not of the sun nor moon but the light of the Lamb slain from the beginning of the world. We also learn of the condition of entering into the gates of that Heavenly Jerusalem: "There shall not enter into it anything defiled, or that worketh abomination, or maketh a lie, but they that are written in the book of life of the Lamb" (Rev 21:27).

Justice demands that nothing unclean, but only the pure of heart shall stand before the face of a pure God. If there were no Purgatory, then the Justice of God would be too terrible for words, for who are they who would dare assert themselves pure enough and spotless enough to stand before the Immaculate Lamb of God? The martyrs who sprinkled the sands of the Coliseum with their blood in testimony of their faith? Most certainly! The missionaries like Paul who spend themselves and are spent for the spread of the Gospel? Most assuredly! The cloistered saints who in the quiet calm of a voluntary Calvary become martyrs without recognition? Most truly!

But these are glorious exceptions. How many millions there are who die with their souls stained with venial sin, who have known evil, and by their strong resolve have drawn from it only to carry with them the weakness of their past as a leaden weight!

The day we were baptized, the Church laid upon us a white garment with the injunction: "Receive this white garment which mayest thou carry without stain before the judgment seat of Our Lord Jesus Christ that thou mayest have life everlasting." How many of us during life have kept that garment unspotted and unsoiled by sin so that we might enter immediately upon death into the white-robed army of the King?

How many souls departing this life have the courage to say that they left it without any undue attachment to creatures and that they were never guilty of a wasted talent, a slight cupidity, an uncharitable deed, a neglect of holy inspiration or even an idle word for which every one of us must render an account? How many souls there are gathered in at the deathbed, like late-season flowers, that are absolved from sins, but not from the debt of their sins?

Take any of our national heroes, whose names we venerate and whose deeds we emulate. Would any Englishman or American who knew something of the Purity of God, as much as he loves and respects the virtues of a Lord Nelson or a George Washington, really believe that either of them at death was free enough from slight faults to enter immediately into the presence of God? Why, the very nationalism of a Nelson or a Washington, which made them both heroes in war, might in a way make them suspect of being unsuited the second after death for that true internationalism of Heaven, where there is neither English nor American, Jew nor Greek, Barbarian nor Free, but all one in Christ Jesus Our Lord.

All these souls who die with some love of God possessing them are beautiful souls, but if there be no Purgatory, then because of their slight imperfections they must be rejected without pity by Divine Justice. Take away Purgatory, and God could not pardon so easily, for will an act of contrition at the edge of the tomb atone for thirty years of sinning? Take away Purgatory and the infinite Justice of God would surely reject from Heaven those who resolve to pay their debts, but have not yet paid the last farthing.

So, I say, Purgatory is where the Love of God tempers the Justice of God, for there God pardons because He has time to retouch these souls with His Cross, to recut them with the chisel of suffering, that they might fit into the great spiritual edifice of the Heavenly Jerusalem, to plunge them into that purifying place where they might wash their stained baptismal robes to be fit to enter into the spotless purity of Heaven; to resurrect them like the phoenix of old from the ashes of their own sufferings so that, like wounded eagles healed by the magic touch of God's cleansing flames, they might mount heavenward to the city of the pure, where Christ is King and Mary is Queen, for, regardless of how trivial the fault, God does not pardon without tears, and there are no tears in Heaven.

On the other hand, Purgatory is a place not only where the Love of God tempers the Justice of God, but where the love of man may temper the injustice of man. I believe that most men and women are quite unconscious of the injustice, the ingratitude, and the thanklessness of their lives until the cold hand of death is laid upon one that they love. It is then, and only then, that they realize (and, oh, with what regret!) the haunting poverty of their love and kindness.

One of the reasons why the bitterest of tears are shed over graves is because of words left unsaid and deeds left undone. "The child never knew how much I loved her." "He never knew how much he meant to me." "I never knew how dear he was until he was gone." Such words are the poisoned arrows which cruel death shoots at our hearts from the door of every sepulchre. Oh, then we realize how differently we would have acted if only the departed one could come back again. Tears are shed in vain before eyes that cannot see; caresses are offered without response to arms that cannot embrace; and sighs stir not a heart whose ear is deaf.

Oh, then the anguish for not offering the flowers before death had come and for not sprinkling the incense while the beloved was still alive and for not speaking the kind words that now must die on the very air they cleave. Oh, the sorrow at the thought that we cannot atone for the stinted affection we gave them, for the light answers we returned to their pleading, and for the lack of reverence we showed to one who was perhaps the dearest thing that God had ever given us to know. Alas, too late! It does little good to water last year's crop, to snare the bird that has flown, or to gather the rose that has withered and died.

Purgatory is a place where the Love of God tempers the Justice of God, but also where the love of man tempers the injustice of man, for it enables hearts who are left behind to break the barriers of time and death, to convert unspoken words into prayers, unburned incense into sacrifice, unoffered flowers into alms, and undone acts of kindness into help for eternal life.

Take away Purgatory and how bitter would be our grief for our unkindnesses and how piercing our sorrow for our forgetfulness. Take away Purgatory and how meaningless are our Memorial and Armistice Days, when we venerate the memory of our dead. Take away Purgatory and how empty are our wreaths, our bowed heads, our moments of silence. But if there be a Purgatory, then immediately the bowed head gives way to a bent knee, the moment of silence to a moment of prayer, and the fading wreath to the abiding offering of the sacrifice of that great Hero of heroes, Christ.

Purgatory, then, enables us to atone for our ingratitude because through our prayers, mortifications, and sacrifices, it makes it possible to bring joy and consolation to the ones we love. Love is stronger than death and hence there should be love for those who have gone before us. We are the offspring of their life, the gathered fruit of their labor, the solicitude of their hearts.

Shall death cut off our gratitude, shall the grave stop our love, shall the cold clod prevent the atoning of our ingratitude? The Church assures us that not being able to give more to them in this world, since they are not of it, we can still seek them out in the hands of Divine Justice and give them the assurance of our love, and the purchasing price of their redemption.

Just as the man who dies in debt has the maledictions of his creditors following him to the grave, but may have his good name restored and revered by the labor of his son who pays the last penny, so, too, the soul of a friend who has gone to death owing a debt of penance to God may have it remitted by us who are left behind, by minting the gold of daily actions into the spiritual coin which purchases redemption.

Into the crucibles of God these departed souls go like stained gold to have their dross burned away by the flames of love. These souls, who have not died in enmity with God, but have fallen wounded on the battlefield of life fighting for the victory of His cause, have not the strength to bind their own wounds and heal their own scars: it remains for us who are still strong and healthy, clad with the armor of faith and the shield of salvation, to heal their wounds and make them whole that they might join the ranks of the victors and march in the procession of the conquerors. We may be sure that if the penny that gives bread to the hungry body delivers a soul to the Table of Our Lord, it will never forget us when it enters into the homeland of victory.

While yet confined to that prison of purifying fire, they hear the voices of the angels and saints who call them to their true fatherland, but they are incapable of breaking their chains, for their time of merit is passed.

Certainly God cannot be unmindful of a wife who offers her merits to the captive soul of a husband waiting for his deliverance. Surely the mercy of God cannot be such that He should be deaf to the good works of a mother who offers them for the liberation of her offspring who are yet stained with the sins of the world. Surely God will not forbid such communication of the living with the dead, since the act of Redemption has guaranteed such a transferring of merits through Christ.

Responsive, then, will we be to the plea not only of our relatives and friends, but of that great mass of unarmed warriors of the Church Suffering who are yet wearing the ragged remnants of sin, but who, in their anxiety of soul to be clothed in the royal robes fit for entrance into the Palace of the King, cry out to our responsive hearts the plaintive and tender plea: "Have mercy on me, have mercy on me, at least you, my friends, for the hand of the Lord has touched me."

CHAPTER TEN

The Hell There Is

Why do moderns deny hell? Because they deny sin. If you deny human guilt, then you must deny the right of a state to judge a criminal, and the further right to sentence him to prison. Once you deny the sovereignty of law, you must necessarily deny punishment. Once you deny the sovereignty of God, you must deny hell.

The basic reason why moderns disbelieve in hell is because they really disbelieve in freedom and responsibility. To believe in hell is to assert that the consequences of good and bad acts are not indifferent. It does make a tremendous amount of difference to your body if you drink tea or TNT, and it makes a greater difference if your soul drinks virtue or vice.

It is as difficult to make a free nation without judges and prisons, as it is to make a free world without Judgment and hell. No State constitution could exist for six months on the basis of a Liberal Christianity which denies that Christ meant what He said: "Depart from me, you cursed, into everlasting fire which was prepared for the devil and his angels" (Mt 25:41).

The modern man also denies hell because he fears his own conscience. Have you ever noticed that saints fear hell but never deny it; and that great sinners deny hell but never fear it? The modern man is accommodating a creed to the way he lives, rather than the way he lives to a creed. The Devil is never so strong as when he gets man to deny there is a devil. So long as he succeeds in getting materialists and sceptics to paint him in red tights with an arrowed tail, and carrying a long pitchfork, he has doped them to the forgetfulness of the great and overwhelming truth that he is a fallen angel.

The modern man who is not living according to his conscience wants a religion without a Cross, a Christ without a Calvary, a Kingdom without Justice, and in his church a "soft dean who never mentions hell to ears polite".

Let not those who profess to be Christian, or who limit Christianity to the Sermon on the Mount, forget that Our Lord closed that sermon with these words: "Every tree that bringeth not forth good fruit, shall be cut down, and shall be cast into the fire. Wherefore by their fruits you shall know them. Not every one that saith to me, Lord, Lord, shall enter into the kingdom of heaven: but he that doth the will of my Father who is in heaven, he shall enter into the kingdom of heaven. Many will say to me in that day: Lord, Lord, have we not prophesied in thy name, and cast out devils in thy name, and done many miracles in thy name? And then will I profess unto them, I never knew you: depart from me, you that work iniquity" (Mt 7:19–23).

Again Our Lord said: "And if thy hand scandalize thee, cut it off: it is better for thee to enter into life, maimed, than having two hands to go into hell, into unquenchable fire: Where their worm dieth not, and the fire is not extinguished. And if thy foot scandalize thee, cut it off. It is better for thee to enter lame into life everlasting, than having two feet, to be cast into the hell of unquenchable fire: Where their worm dieth not, and the fire is not extinguished. And if thy eye scandalize thee, pluck it out. It is better for thee with one eye to enter into the kingdom of God, than having two eyes to be cast into the hell of fire: Where their worm dieth not, and the fire is not extinguished. For every one shall be salted with fire: and every victim shall be salted with salt" (Mk 9:42–48).

Why do souls go to hell? In the last analysis, they go to hell for only one reason: because they refuse to love. Souls do not go to hell just because they break the commandments, for why should the breaking of a commandment merit hell? God does not forbid lying, murder, dishonesty, adultery, to amuse Himself. They are not arbitrary commands. He forbids them because they hurt us. Their violation is a sign of our anti-love.

The Commandments of God are like a book of directions that comes with a gadget. You disobey them;

you get no results. Why, then, if you are unhappy by disobeying the set of directions of One who loves you, do you say God is cruel? Hell is not a defect of God's love. Hell is a state of those who refuse to have God's love, when He offers it. Just as Heaven is the undeniable blessedness won by the wholly selfless and loving, so hell is the undeniable cursedness won by the wholly self-centered or hateful. Heaven is community; hell is loneliness.

What is the nature of the punishment of hell? It is twofold because it corresponds to the double character of sin. Every mortal sin consists in a turning away from God and a turning to creatures. Because we turn away from God, we feel the absence of His Love, His Beauty, His Truth—and this is called the pain of loss. Because we turn to creatures and pervert them to our sinful purposes, we are punished in some way by the very creatures that we abused. Hell fire is one of the aspects of this pain of sense.

This pain of sense is an exemplification of the principle that the punishment fits the crime. If you disobey one of nature's laws, you suffer a corresponding retribution. If you become intoxicated some night and put yourself in a state of amiable incandescence, you do not necessarily wake up the next morning with an overdrawn bank account. But you do feel the effects of abusing the God-given thirst by something vaguely described as a "hangover". In almost so many words the alcohol says to you: "I was made by God to be used by you as a reasonable creature. You perverted me from the purpose God intended. Now since I am on God's side, not yours, I shall abuse you, because you abused me."

For every action, there is always a contrary, an equal, reaction. "With traitorous trueness and loyal deceit. In faith to Him, their fickleness to me." Nature refuses to be our servant because we refuse to accept Our Master. Hence, there will be different kinds of punishment in hell. The fiercer the grip sinful pleasures had on a soul in this life, the more fiercely will the fires torment it in eternity. Do not try to escape this logic or blind yourself to Divine Authority by arguing that hell could not be as you have heard some preachers picture it. I am only saying: Do not reject the truth of the book because the pictures are bad.

From three distinct points of view, the pain of loss is best understood as the loss of Divine Love. Hell is a place where there is no love, for God is Love.

Hell is the hatred of the things you love. A sailor lost on a raft at sea loves water. He was made for it, and water was made for him. He knows that he *ought not* to drink the water from the sea, but he violates the dictates of his reason. The result is, he is now more thirsty than before, even thirsty when he is the most filled. He hates water as poison; at the same time he is mad with the thirst for it.

In like manner, the soul was made to live on the love of God, but if it perverts that love by salting it with sin, then as the sailor hates the very water be drinks, so the soul hates the perverted love it seeks. It then hates the very thing it desires, namely, the love of God. It despises the very love it craves; it abominates the very love it needs. As the insane hate most the very persons whom in their saner moments they really love the most, so the damned in hell hate God Whom they were really meant to love above all things.

They become like wandering comets who every now and then approach the sun, their true center, and then swing away from the light into incredible darkness. The wicked do not want hell because they enjoy its torments; they want hell because they do not want God. They *need* God, but they do not want Him. Hell is eternal suicide for hating love. Hell is the hatred of the God you love.

Hell is the mind eternally mad at itself for wounding love. How often during life you have said: "I hate myself." No one who ever condemned you could add to the consciousness of your guilt. You knew it a thousand times better than they. When did you hate yourself most? Certainly not when you failed to act on a tip on the stock market. You hated yourself most when you hurt someone whom you loved. You even said: "I can never forgive myself for doing that."

The souls in hell hate themselves most for wounding Perfect Love, as you might hate yourself all your life for hurting one whom you loved. They can never forgive themselves for hurting Love. Hence their hell is eternal: eternal self-imposed unforgiveness. It is not that God would not forgive them. It is rather they will not forgive themselves. On earth they were selfish, not loving. In hell that selfishness is consummated and eternalized. It is the madhouse of the incurables who hate themselves for hating the Physician of their souls, the place where the mind turns against itself because it turned from God.

How often in this world the sight of moral beauty arouses indignation! The evil person incessantly wants a recasting of all values. Put one good boy in a gang of boys that spends its time in petty thievery or breaking school windows, and the chances are the gang will turn against that good boy, ridicule his moral principles, tell him he is a coward or old-fashioned. Exactly that same mentality is present in adult life. Whenever a professor attacks morality and makes fun of religion before his pupils, you can be sure nine times out of ten that his life is rotten.

Goodness is a reproach to such persons: they want everyone to be like themselves, so no one can reproach their conscience. This revolt against goodness and truth is the basic cause of the persecution and mockery of religion. Now if such things are possible to corrupt souls on earth, why should they not be possible in eternity? They will still hate Love because hate has nothing in common with Love. They reject the one remedy that could have helped them, the love of Someone besides themselves.

Hell is submission to Love under Justice. We are free in this world; we can no more be forced to love God than we can be forced to love classical music, antiques, swing bands, olives, or Bach. Force and love are contraries. Love and freedom are correlative.

When you came into this world, God said: "I ask you to love me freely that you may be perfect." Suppose we freely say: "I refuse to love truth and justice and beauty or my neighbor. I shall love error, and graft, and ugliness." Later on, you die in that state. But you do not escape that Divine Love, which you abused, any more than the traitor escapes the country whose love he despised.

Either you possess love, or love possesses you. In marriage a man and woman were meant to possess love, but that love can be perverted so that in the end, love possesses them. How often a husband, for example, tied to a woman by marriage is possessed by her, by her wants, her selfishness, and her jealousies. Often, too, many a wife is tied to a drunkard or worthless husband until death do them part. They do not freely love one another; they are *forced* in virtue of the justice of their contracts to love one another until death do them part. To be forced to love anyone is hell.

The lost souls could have loved God freely, but they chose to rebel against that love and in doing so came under Divine Justice, as the criminal falls from the love of a country to its justice. They do not possess love; love possesses them. Justice forces them to *love* God, that is, to submit to the Divine Order; but to be forced to *love* is the very negation of love. It is hell! Hell is a place where Love possesses you in justice, but where you do not possess love.

Think not that hell ever ends, or that some day the damned go to Heaven. If a soul in hell went to Heaven, Heaven to it would be a hell. Suppose you hated higher mathematics; suppose your morning paper had nothing in it but logarithms; suppose everyone you met talked to you about Space-Time differentials; every broadcast you heard was on the theory of relativity; every book you read was on the subject of pointer-readings. After a while, mathematics would drive you mad. Now the souls in hell hate Perfect Life, Perfect Truth, and Perfect Love—which is God—and if they had to live with that which they hated more than you hate mathematics, then God would be their great punishment, as mathematics would be yours. Heaven would be hell.

Hell must be eternal. What is one thing life can never forgive? Death, because death is the negation of life. What is the one thing that Truth can never forgive? Error, for error is its contradiction. What is the one thing that Love can never forgive? It is the refusal to love, for hate would be the destruction and annihilation of love. That is why hell is eternal—it is the negation of Love.

Everything does not come out right in the end, for we cannot at one moment believe that we are saved by doing God's Will, and the next moment believe that it has no significance. Somehow or other, there comes to mind the final picture of mankind: the Divine Judge in the center, the sheep on the right going to Heaven, and the goats on the left going to hell. Where the tree falls, there it lies.

You ask: "How can God be so wrathful as to sentence souls to hell?" Remember that God does not sentence us to hell, as much as we sentence ourselves. When the cage is opened, the bird flies out to that which it loved; when our body dies, we fly out, either to an Eternity of love of God or to a hatred of God.

God has not a different mood for those who go to hell than for those who go to Heaven. The difference is in us, not in Him. We attribute anger and wrath to Him only because we feel His Justice as anger. Every criminal thinks that the judge has got something against him. The same justice of the judge could free him if the criminal were innocent. Then he would think the judge was kind. The sun which shines on wax softens it; the sun which shines on mud hardens it. There is no difference in the sun, but only in that upon which it shines. So there is no difference in the God of Love when He judges the wicked and the saved; the difference is in those whom He judges.

We must, therefore, get out of our heads the idea that God is mad with us when we hurt ourselves. God is never offended against us because we sin against Him, as if He were a monarch to be obeyed. We never offend

God except when we do something that is contrary to our own good, or better, when we hurt ourselves. Life is important. It only takes a second for a man to lose his leg by carelessness, but he has lost it for all time. It only takes a lifetime to commit a sin, but we can lose Heaven forever. God is a loving Father indeed, and He accepts us back as He did the Prodigal, but only on condition that we are repentant.

Hell is at the foot of the Hill of Calvary; and no one of us can go down to hell without first passing over the Hill where there is a God-man enthroned with arms outstretched to embrace, head bent to kiss, and heart open to love. I do not find it hard to understand God preparing a hell for those who want to hate themselves eternally for having hated Him. But I do find it hard to understand why that same God should die upon a Cross to save unworthy me from a hell which my sins so rightly deserve.

CHAPTER ELEVEN

Heaven

It is not often nowadays that men speak of eternity; their thoughts are almost always on time. In fact, time has become one of the most important things in the world. Some years ago, before physics became the fashionable science, the human mind was wont to conceive of time as something in which things happened. Now, it is looked upon as the very fabric of the universe. Sacred Scripture tells us that a moment will come when there will be no more time. The unsacred scripture of our day tells us that time is the very essence of things.

Would we seek for evidences of this mood of temporalism, we could find them in every nook and corner of the world today. In the field of morals, for example, the current doctrine is that any action is moral, provided the time in which we live regards it as moral.

Religion, too, has drunk deep of the intoxicating draughts of temporalism, and now, reeling under its effects, it preaches a religion wholly confined to time, utterly oblivious of eternity. It no longer asks a man to save his soul for eternity; it asks him to save his body for time. It is unconcerned about citizenship in the Kingdom of God, but tremendously excited about citizenship in the Kingdom of Time. That is, incidentally, why some modern religions stress birth control, favoring as they do the economic motive that belongs to time, rather than the religious motive which belongs to eternity.

Philosophy, likewise, has become so obsessed with that notion that it teaches with unbuttoned pride that there is no such thing as Truth with a capital "T", for truth is ambulatory: we make it as we go; it depends on the time in which we live. There are not wanting even writers who have gone to the excess of saying that God is not in eternity, but is in time, or rather He is being produced by whole cosmic floods of time, undergoing miraculous baptisms at the hands of time, and being hurled onward and forward to some goal which is not yet certain, but which time will reveal if we ever give it time enough.

The Church is not in sympathy with this mood of temporalism. She teaches that it is about time that we cease talking about time, and begin to think of the timeless. I, therefore, propose to prove the superiority of the Church's attitude over that of the modern world by showing first of all that time stands in the way of real happiness, and secondly, that only insofar as we succeed in transcending time do we ever begin to be happy.

Time is the one thing that makes real pleasure impossible, for the simple reason that it does not permit us to make a club sandwich of pleasures. By its very nature, it forbids us to have many pleasures together under the penalty of having none of them at all. By the mere fact that I exist in time, it is impossible for me to combine the pleasures of marching with the old guard of Napoleon, and at the same time, advancing under the flying eagles of Caesar.

By the mere fact that I live in time, I cannot enjoy simultaneously the winter sports of the Alps and the limpid waters of the Riviera. Time makes it impossible for me to be stirred by the oratory of a Demosthenes and at the same time to listen to the melodious accents of the great Bossuet. Time does not permit me to combine the prudence that comes with age and the buoyancy that belongs to youth. It is the one thing that prevents me from gathering around the same festive board with Aristotle, Socrates, Thomas Aquinas, and Mercier in order to learn the secrets of great minds in solving the riddles of a universe.

If it were not for time, Dante and Shakespeare could have sipped tea together, and Homer even now might tell us his stories in English. It is all very nice and lovely to enjoy the mechanical perfections of this age of luxury, but there are moments when I would like to enjoy the calm and peace of the Middle Ages, but time will not permit it. If I live in the twentieth century, I must sacrifice the pleasures of the thirteenth, and if I enjoy the Athenian age of Pericles, I must be denied the Florentine age of Dante.

Thus it is that time makes it impossible to combine pleasures. I know there are advertisements that would invite us to dine and dance, but no one can do both comfortably at one and the same time. All things are good, and yet none can be enjoyed except in their season, and the enjoyment must always be tinged with the regret that time will demand their surrender. Time gives me things, but it also takes them away. When it does give, it gives but singly, and thus life becomes but just one fool thing after another.

This thought suggests the suspicion that if time makes the combination of pleasures impossible, then if I could ever transcend time, I might, in some way, increase my happiness, and this I find to be true, for every conscious desire to prolong a pleasure is a desire to make it an enduring "now". Like cats before the fire, we want to prolong the pleasure indefinitely; we want it to be permanent and not successive.

Go back in the storehouse of your memory, and you will find ample proof that it is always in those moments when you are least conscious of the passing of time that you most thoroughly enjoy its pleasures. How often it happens, for example, when listening to an absorbing conversation or the thrilling experiences of a much traveled man, that the hours pass by so quickly we are hardly conscious of them, and we say: "The time passes like everything." What is true of a delightful conversation is also true of aesthetic pleasures.

I dare say that very few listening to an orchestra translate the beauty of one of Beethoven's overtures would ever notice the passing of time. In just the proportion that it pleases and thrills, the orchestra makes us unconscious of how long we were absorbed by its melodies. The contrary fact illustrates the same truth. The more we notice time, the less we are being interested.

If our friends keep looking at their watches while we tell a story, we can be very sure that they are being bored by our story. A man who keeps his eye on the clock is not the man who is interested in his work. The more we notice the passing of time, the less is our pleasure, and the less we notice the passing of time, the greater is our pleasure.

These psychological facts of experience testify that not only is time the obstacle of enjoyment, but escape from it is the essential of happiness. Suppose we could enlarge upon our experience in such a way as to imagine ourselves completely outside of time and succession, in a world where there would never be a "before" nor an "after", but only a "now".

Suppose we could go out to another existence where the great pleasures of history would not be denied us because of their historical incompatibility, but all unified in a beautiful hierarchic order, like a pyramid in that all would minister to the very unity of our personality. Suppose I say that I could reach a point of timelessness at which all the enjoyments and beauties and happinesses of time could be reduced to those three fundamental unities that constitute the perfection of our being, namely, Life, Truth, and Love, for into these three all pleasures can be resolved.

Suppose first of all that I could reduce to a single focal point all the pleasures of life, so that in the "now" which never looked before nor after, I could enjoy the life that seems to be in the sea when its restless bosom is dimpled with calm, as well as the urge of life that seems to be in all the hill-encircling brooks that loiter to the sea; the life which provokes the dumb, dead sod to tell its thoughts in violets; the life which pulsates through a springtime blossom as the swinging cradle for the fruit.

Suppose that I could enjoy the life of the flowers as they open the chalice of their perfume to the sun; the life of the birds as the great heralds of song and messengers of joy; the life of all the children that run shouting to their mothers' arms; the life of all the parents that beget a life like unto their own; and the life of the mind that on the wings of an invisible thought strikes out to the hid battlements of eternity—to the life whence all living comes.

Suppose that, in addition to concentrating all the life of the universe in a single point, I could also concentrate in another focal point all the truths of the world, so that

I could know the truth the astronomer seeks as he looks up through his telescope; the truth the biologist seeks as he looks down through his microscope; the truth about the heavens, and who shut up the sea with doors when it did burst forth as issuing from a womb; the truth about the hiding place of darkness and the treasure house of hail, and the cave of the winds.

Suppose that I could know the truth about the common things: why fire, like a spirit, mounts to the heavens heavenly, and why gold, like clay, falls to the earth earthly; the truth the philosopher seeks as he tears apart with his mind the very wheels of the universe; the truth the theologian seeks as he uses Revelation to unravel the secrets of God, which far surpass anything the greatest minds, unaided by Revelation, can ever dream of.

Suppose that over and above all these pleasures of life and truth, there could be unified in another focal point all the delights and beauties of love that have contributed to the happiness of the universe: the love of the patriot for his country; the love of the soldier for his cause; the love of the scientist for his discovery; the love of the flowers as they smile upon the sun; the love of the earth at whose breast all creation drinks the milk of life.

Suppose you could unify at that same point the love of mothers, who swing open the great portals of life that a child may see the light of day; the love of friend for friend to whom he could reveal his heart through words; the love of spouse for spouse; the love of husband for wife; and even the love of angel for angel, and the angel for God with a fire and heat sufficient to enkindle the hearts of ten thousand times ten thousand worlds.

Suppose that all the pleasures of the world could be brought to these three focal points of life and truth and love, just as the rays of the sun are brought to unity in the sun; and suppose that all the successive pleasures of time could be enjoyed at one and the same "now"; and suppose that these points of unity on which our hearts and minds and souls would be directed, would not merely be three abstractions, but that the focal point in which all the pleasures of life were concentrated would be a life personal enough to be a Father.

Suppose that that focal point of truth, in which all the pleasures of truth were concentrated, would not merely be an abstract truth, but a truth personal enough to be a Word or a Son, and that that focal point of love, in which all the pleasures of love were concentrated, would be not merely an abstract love, but a love personal enough to be a Holy Spirit.

Suppose that once elevated to that supreme height, happiness would be so freed from limitations that it would include these three as one, not in succession, but with a permanence; not as in time, but as in the timeless—then we would have eternity, then we would have God! The Father, Son, and Holy Ghost: Perfect Life, Perfect Truth, Perfect Love. Then we would have happiness—and that would be Heaven.

But will the pleasures of that timelessness with God and that enjoyment of life and truth and love, which is the Trinity, be in any way comparable to the pleasures of time? Is there anyone on this earth who will tell me about Heaven? Certainly there are three faculties to which one might appeal, namely, to what one has seen, to what one has heard, and to what one can imagine.

Will Heaven surpass all the pleasures of the eye, and the ear, and the imagination? First of all, will it be as beautiful as some of the things that can be seen? I have seen the Villa d'Este of Rome with its long lanes of ilex and laurel, and its great avenues of cypress trees, all full of what might be called the vivacity of quiet and living silence; I have seen a sunset on the Mediterranean when two clouds came down like pillars to form a brilliant red tabernacle for the sun and it glowing like a golden host.

I have seen, from the harbor, the towers and the minarets of Constantinople pierce through the mist that hung over them like a silken veil; I have seen the chateau country of France and her Gothic cathedrals aspiring heavenward like prayers; I have seen the beauties of the castles of the Rhine, and the combination of all these visions almost makes me think of the doorkeeper of the Temple of Diana who used to cry out to those who entered: "Take heed to your eye", and so I wonder if the things of eternity will be as beautiful as the combined beauty of all the things which I have seen....

I have not seen all the beauties of nature, others I have heard of that I have not seen: I have heard of the beauties of the hanging gardens of Babylon, of the pomp and dignity of the palaces of the Doges, of the brilliance and glitter of the Roman Forum as its foundations rocked with the tramp of Rome's resistless legions; I have heard of the splendor of the Temple of Jerusalem as it shone like a jewel in the morning sun.

I have heard of the beauties of the garden of Paradise where fourfold rivers flowed through lands rich with the gold and onyx, a garden made beautiful as only God knows how to make a beautiful garden; I have heard of countless other beauties and joys of nature that tongue cannot describe, nor touch of brush convey, and I wonder if all the joys and pleasures of Heaven will be as great as the combined beauty of all the things of which I have heard.

Beyond what I have heard and seen, there are things that I can imagine: I can imagine a world in which there never would be pain, disease, or death; I can imagine a world wherein every man would live in a castle, and in that commonwealth of castles there would be a due order of justice without complaint or anxiety.

I can imagine a world in which the winter would never come, and in which the flowers would never fade, and the sun would never set; I can imagine a world in which there would always be a peace and a quiet without idleness, a profound knowledge of things without research, a constant enjoyment without satiety; I can imagine a world that would eliminate all the evils and diseases and worries of life, and combine all its best joys and happiness; and I wonder if all the happiness of Heaven would be like the happiness of earth which I can imagine.

Will eternity be anything like what I have seen, or what I have heard, or what I can imagine? No, eternity will be nothing like anything I have seen, heard, or imagined. Listen to the voice of God: "That eye hath not seen, nor ear heard, neither hath it entered into the heart of man, what things God hath prepared for them that love him" (1 Cor 2:9).

CHAPTER TWELVE

Faith

Regardless of your religious background, you have doubtless observed the tremendous disparity of points of view between those who possess Divine Faith through God's grace and those who have it not. Have you ever noticed when discussing important subjects, as pain, sorrow, sin, happiness, marriage, children, education, the purpose of life, and the meaning of death, that the Catholic point of view is now poles apart from what is called the modern view?

You who have the faith probably have often felt a sense of inadequacy in dealing with those who have no faith, as if there were no common denominator. You and that person without faith seem to be living in different worlds. You feel powerless to penetrate the natural mentality of the modern pagan whom you meet on the street. It is like telling a blind man about color. You are not talking the same language. Like workmen on the Tower of Babel, there is no common understanding.

It was not so many years ago that those who rejected many Christian truths were considered off the reservation; for example, the divorced who remarried, the atheists, the enemies of the family, or those who held that law was a dictate of the will, not of reason. Today, it is we who are considered off the reservation. It is they who are on it. The Christian is today on the defensive if for no other reason than because he is the exception.

The clarity of vision and certitude of those who have the gift of faith is sometimes misunderstood even by those who have faith. Hence, a Catholic is sometimes impatient with one who has not the faith, wrongly thinking that the reason he sees the truth so clearly is because of his own innate cleverness, and the reason his neighbor does not see it is due either to his stupidity or his stubbornness. Faith, it must be remembered, is not due to our wisdom, and the lack of faith is not due to their ignorance. Faith is solely a gift of God. "Flesh and blood hath not revealed it to thee, but my Father who is in heaven" (Mt 16:17).

If you have not the faith, have you not often considered as utterly foolish, absurd, and superstitious the judgments, the philosophy of life, and the outlook of those who live by faith? You think a Catholic, for instance, has surrendered both his freedom and his reason by obeying the laws of the Church and by accepting the truth of Christ in His Church.

Your judgment, then, is very much like one who looks at the windows of a church from outside, where they seem to be a meaningless confusion of leaden lines and dull colors. Once inside the church, and the leaden lines fade away as the pattern reveals itself vibrant with colors and life. In like manner, the Church may seem bewildering to those who are outside, but once you enter it, you will discover an order and harmony and a "beauty that leaves all other beauty pain".

The world today seems much more united in its negation of belief, than in its acceptance of a belief. The older generation could give you at least ten reasons for a wrong belief, such as a belief in materialism, but the modern man cannot give even one bad reason for total unbelief.

It is shockingly true that there is more in common today between a Christian in the state of grace and an Orthodox Jew or a Mohammedan than there is between the true Christian and the average so-called Christian person you are apt to meet at a nightclub, or even at the table in your neighbor's house.

When the Christian talks about God, the Orthodox Jew or Mohammedan can understand him, for they, too, believe that God is Sovereign and Judge of all men. But to the average pagan who believes man came from beast and, therefore, must act like one, all this is as so much fatuous nonsense and senile stupidity. A striking confirmation of this is that in the face of Anti-God crusades of Russia, Christians, Jews, and Moslems presented a common front.

Why this difference between those who have the faith, and those who have it not? It is due to the fact that a soul in the state of grace has its intellect illumined, which enables it to perceive new truths which otherwise would be beyond its powers. Divine grace supernaturalizes that which makes us human, namely, our intellect and our will, giving them the power of higher action. The intellect still continues to know truth, but through grace operating in it as faith, it knows higher truths than those of reason. The human will, in like manner, retains its love of good, but by grace operating on it, it can now rely more on God or love Him more than by its unaided efforts:

	Faculty	Theological Virtues	Action	Object
Soul	{ Intellect	Faith	To believe	God
	{ Will	{ Hope	To hope	God
		{ Charity	To love	God

You have exactly the same eyes at night as you have in the day, but you cannot see at night, because you lack the additional light of the sun. So, too, let two minds with identically the same education, the same mental capacities, and the same judgment, look on a Host enthroned on an altar. The one sees bread, the other sees Christ, not, of course, with the eyes of the flesh, but with the eyes of faith. Let them both look on death: one sees the end of a biological entity, the other an immortal creature being judged by God on how it used its freedom. The reason for the difference is: one has a light that the other lacks, namely, the light of faith.

This light of faith operates on human problems somewhat like an X ray. You look at a box with the naked eye and it appears to be of wood and tinsel and cheap wrapping paper, and, therefore, of no great value. You look at it later with an X ray and you see the contents of the box to be diamonds and rubies. In like manner, those who live only by the light of reason gaze upon a sick and feverish body, and see pain as valueless as a curse. But the mind endowed with the extra light of faith, sees through the pain: to him it is either a means for reparation for sins, or a stepping stone to greater unity with His Master, whom "Life made love, and love made pain, and pain made death".

If you have not the light of faith, you may be very educated, but can you correlate your knowledge into a unified philosophy of life? Does your psychology jibe with your ethics? Does your emphasis on the dignity of man click with your denial of a soul? Rather is not your mind like a flattened Japanese lantern, a riot of colors without pattern or purpose? What you need to do is to have the candle of faith lighted on the inside of that lantern that you may see all your different lines of knowledge meet into one absorbing pattern leading to God.

Education is not the condition of receiving this additional light of faith, although an educated person can understand the faith better. Since the light of faith is from God and not from us, we cannot supply it, any more than we can restore vision if we lose our eyes. Being a true Christian, therefore, does not require an education. *It is an education!*

A little child who today is telling a sister in school that God made him, that he was made to know, love, and serve God, and to be happy with Him in the next world, knows more, and is more profoundly educated, than all the professors throughout the length and breadth of this land, who babble about space-time deities, who prattle about new ethics to fit unethical lives, who negate all morality to suit their immoral thinking, but who do not know, therefore, that beyond time is the timeless, beyond space is the spaceless, the Infinite Lord and Master of the Universe.

No wonder Our Lord prayed: "I confess to thee, O Father, Lord of heaven and earth, because thou hast hidden these things from the wise and prudent, and hast revealed them to little ones. Yea, Father, for so it hath seemed good in thy sight" (Lk 10:21). St. Paul later on clearly distinguished between these two kinds of wisdom: the false wisdom which uses reason to negate the God who gave reason, and the higher wisdom born of the grace of God: "For the foolishness of God is wiser than men; and the weakness of God is stronger than men" (1 Cor 1:25).

That is why those who live by the higher light of faith are so insistent that education be religious for, after all, if one does not know *why* he is living, there is not much purpose in living. There are those who would suggest that there be no religious training until the child is old enough to "decide for himself". They should also consistently suggest a child in a slum should not be removed to a better environment until he is old enough to decide for himself. Unfortunately, when that time comes he may already have contracted tuberculosis. Why not also argue that no infant should be born into the world until he is old enough to decide who his parents should be, to what economic class he will belong, and to what code he will subscribe, or even to decide whether he wants to come into the world at all.

Though faith is a gift of God, and though God will give it to those that ask it, there is one very human obstacle why more minds do not receive it, and that is pride. Pride is the commonest sin of the modern mind, and yet the one of which the modern mind is never conscious. You have heard people say: "I like drink too much", or "I am quick-tempered", but did you ever hear anyone say: "I am conceited"?

Pride is the exaltation of self as an absolute standard of truth, goodness, and morality. It judges everything by itself, and for that reason everyone else is a rival, particularly God. Pride makes it impossible to know God. If I know everything, then not even God can teach me anything. If I am filled with myself, then there is no place for God. Like the innkeepers of Bethlehem, we say to the Divine Visitor: "There is no room."

Pride is of two kinds: it is either the pride of omniscience or the pride of nescience. The pride of omniscience tries to convince your neighbor you know everything; the new pride of nescience tries to convince your neighbor that he knows nothing. The latter is the technique used by "sophomores" who pride themselves on the fact that man can know nothing. Hence, they doubt everything, and of this they are very sure. They seem to forget that the doubting of everything is impossible, for doubt is a shadow, and there can be no shadow without light.

If pride is the great human obstacle to faith, it follows that, from the human side, the essential condition of receiving faith is humility. Humility is not an underestimation of what we are, but the plain, unadulterated truth. A man who is six feet tall is not humble if he says: "No, really, I am only five feet tall."

If there ever came a moment in your life when you admitted you did not know it all, or said: "Oh! What a fool am I", you created a vacuum and a void which God's grace could fill. Before you accept the gift of faith, there may be a moment when you will think that you are giving up your reason; but that is only seeming, not real.

Your eye does not constantly look out at the light. Every few seconds it blinks, that is, it goes into temporary darkness; the blink apparently destroys vision. Really, the blink is the condition of better vision. So with your reason in relation to faith. There comes a time in conversion when you blink on your reason, that is, you doubt about its capacity to know everything, and you affirm the possibility that God could enlighten you. Then comes the gift of faith. Once that is received, you find out that instead of destroying your reason, you have perfected it. Faith now becomes to your reason what a telescope is to your eye; it opens up new fields of vision and new worlds that before were hidden and unknown.

Think not either that you lose your freedom by accepting the faith. A few years ago, I received a letter from a radio listener who said: "I imagine that you from your earliest youth were surrounded by priests and nuns who never permitted you to think for yourself. Why not throw off the yoke of Rome and begin to be free?"

I answered him thus: "In the center of a sea was an island on which children played and danced and sang. Around that island were great high walls which had stood for centuries. One day, some strange men came to the island in individual rowboats, and said to the children: Who put up these walls? Can you not see that they are destroying your freedom? Tear them down!

"The children tore them down! Now if you go there, you will find all the children huddled together in the center of the island, afraid to play, afraid to sing, afraid to dance—afraid of falling into the sea."

Faith is not a dam which prevents the flow of the river of reason and thought; it is a levee that prevents unreason from flooding the countryside. Our senses were meant by God to be perfected by reason. That is why a man who loses his reason deliberately by drunkenness no longer sees as well as an animal, nor behaves as well as an animal. We say: "He has lost his senses."

Once the human senses have been deprived of reason, which is their perfection, they no longer function even as well as the sense of an animal. In like manner, once the human reason has lost faith, which is the perfection God freely intended it to have, then reason does not function as well without faith as it does with it. That is why reason alone is unable to get us out of the mess we are in today. Of and by itself, it cannot function well enough to handle the problems created by loss of faith and by misuse of reason and by sin.

The following facts about faith are important:

1. Faith is not believing that something will happen, nor is it the acceptance of what is contrary to reason, nor is it an intellectual recognition that a man might give to something he does not understand or which his reason cannot prove, for example, relativity. Faith

is the acceptance of a truth on the authority of God revealing.

Faith is a supernatural virtue, whereby, inspired and assisted by the grace of God, we believe as true those things He revealed, not because the truth of these things is clearly evident from reason alone, but because of the authority of God, who cannot deceive nor be deceived.

Before faith, one makes an investigation by reason. Just as no businessman would extend you credit without a reason for doing so, neither are you expected to put faith in anyone without a reason. Before you have faith, you study the motives of believing, for example, why should I put faith in Christ?

Your reason investigates the miracles He worked, the prophecies that preannounced Him, and the consonance of His teaching with your reason. These constitute the preambles of faith, from which you form a judgment of credibility: "This truth, that Christ is the Son of God, is worthy of belief." Passing to the practical order, you add: "I must believe it."

From then on, you give your assent: "I believe He is the Son of God, and, this being so, whatever He reveals, I will accept as God's truth." The motive for your assent in faith is always the authority of God, who tells you it is true. You would not believe unless you saw that you must believe.

You believe the truths of reason because there is intrinsic evidence; you believe in the truths of God because there is extrinsic evidence. You believe the sun is ninety-two million miles away from the earth though you never measured it; you believe that Moscow is the capital of Russia though you never saw it. So you accept the Truths of Christianity on the authority of God revealing in His Son Jesus Christ, Our Lord.

Faith, therefore, never is blind. Since your reason is dependent on uncreated Reason or Divine Truth, it follows that your reason should bow down to what God reveals. You believe now, not because of the arguments; they were only a necessary preliminary. You believe because God said it. The torch now burns by its own brilliance.

The nature of the act of faith was revealed by Our Lord's attitude toward the unbelieving Pharisees. They had seen miracles worked and prophecies fulfilled. They were not lacking in motives for belief. But they still refused to believe. Our Lord took a little child in His midst and said: "Amen I say to you, whosoever shall not receive the kingdom of God as a little child, shall not enter into it" (Mk 10:15).

By this He meant that the act of faith has more in common with the trusting belief of a child in his mother than with the assent of a critic. The child believes what the mother tells him because she said it. His belief is an unaffected and trusting homage of love to his mother.

When the Christian believes, he does so, not because he has in the back of his mind the miracles of Christ, but because of the authority of One who can neither deceive nor be deceived. "If we receive the testimony of men, the testimony of God is greater. For this is the testimony of God, which is greater, because he hath testified of his Son. He that believeth in the Son of God, hath the testimony of God in himself. He that believeth not the Son, maketh him a liar; because he believeth not in the testimony which God hath testified of his Son" (1 Jn 5:9–10).

2. You cannot argue, or study, or reason, or hypnotize, or whip yourself, into faith. Faith is a gift of God. When anyone instructs you in Christian doctrine, he does not give you faith. He is only a spiritual agriculturist, tilling the soil of your soul, uprooting a few weeds and breaking up the clods of egotism. It is God who drops the seed. "For by grace you are saved through faith, and that not of yourselves, for it is the gift of God" (Eph 2:8).

If faith were a will to believe, you could produce your own faith by an act of the will. All you can do is to dispose yourself for its reception from the hands of God. As a dry stick is better disposed for burning than a wet stick, so a humble man is better disposed for faith than a know-it-all. In either case, as the fire that burns must come from outside the stick, so your faith must come from outside yourself, namely, from God.

When you try to make everything clear by reason, you somehow only succeed in making everything confusion. Once you introduce a single mystery, everything else becomes clear in the light of that one mystery. The sun is the "mystery" in the universe; it is so bright you cannot look at it; you cannot "see" it. But in the light of it, everything else becomes clear. As Chesterton once said: "But you can see the moon and things under the moon, but the moon is the mother of lunatics."

3. Faith is unique and vital. There are not many faiths. There is only one faith: "One Lord, one faith, one baptism" (Eph 4:5). Out of the millions and millions of men who walked this earth, there is only One who is the Incarnate Lord; out of the millions of lights in the heavens, there is only one sun to light our world. "Upon this rock I will build my Church"—not my churches.

Faith is like life; it must be taken in its entirety. Two mothers appeared in the court of Solomon. Both claimed a babe as their own. Solomon said that he would divide the child and give each claimant a half. One of the women protested and said: "Give the babe to her." Wise Solomon thereupon decided that the babe belonged to the one who protested, for she was the real mother. The Church is like that: it insists on the whole Truth.

Hence, you may not pick and choose among the words of the Blessed Lord and say: "I will accept the Sermon on the Mount, but not your words about hell." Or, "I believe in your doctrine of motherhood, but I cannot accept your teaching that it is unlawful for a man to divorce and marry again." The truths of God are like that babe: it is either the whole babe, or nothing.

Every religion in the world, I care not what it is, contains some reflection of one Eternal Truth. Every philosophy, every world religion, every sect, contains an arc of the perfect round of the Natural and Revealed Truth. Confucianism has the fraction of fellowship; Indian asceticism has the fraction of self-abnegation; each human sect has an aspect of Christ's Truth.

That is why, in approaching those who have not the Faith, one should not begin by pointing out their errors, but rather by indicating the fraction of truth they have in common with the fullness of Truth. Instead of saying to the Confucian: "You are wrong in ignoring the Fatherhood of God", one should say: "You are right in emphasizing brotherhood, but to make your brotherhood perfect, you need the Fatherhood of God and the Sonship of Christ, and the vivifying Unity of the Holy Spirit."

So, with every other religion and sect in the world. Today, men are starving. One should not go to them and say: "Do not eat poisons; they will kill you." We need only to give bread. In religion, in like manner, there is too much emphasis on the errors of unbelievers and not enough on the affirmation of Truth by believers. Break the bread of affirmation and teaching, and the grace of God will do the rest.

This is the great beauty of the Catholic Faith; its sense of proportion, or balance, or should we say, its humor. It does not handle the problem of death to the exclusion of sin; nor the problem of pain to the exclusion of matter; nor the problem of sin, to the exclusion of human freedom; nor the social use of property to the exclusion of personal right; nor the reality of the body and sex to the exclusion of the soul and its function; nor the reality of matter to the forgetfulness of the Spirit.

It never allows one doctrine to go to your head, like wine to an empty stomach. It keeps its balance, for truth is a precarious thing. Like the great rocks in the Alps, there are a thousand angles at which they will fall, but there is only one at which they would stand.

It is easy to be a "pink" in this century, as it was easy to be a "liberal" in the nineteenth; it is easy to be a "materialist" today, as it was easy to be an "idealist" in the nineteenth century, but to keep one's head in the midst of all these changing moods and fancies, so that one is right, not when the world is right, but right when the world is wrong, is the thrill of a tightrope walker, the thrill of the romance of orthodoxy.

4. The acceptance of the fullness of Truth will have the unfortunate quality of making you hated by the world. Forget for a moment the history of Christianity, and the fact that Christ existed. Suppose there appeared in this world today a man who claimed to be Divine Truth;

and who did not say: "I will teach you Truth", but "I am *the Truth*." Suppose he gave evidence by his works of the truth of his statement. Knowing ourselves as we do, with our tendency to relativism, to indifference, and to the fusing of right and wrong, how do you suppose we would react to that Divine Truth? With hatred, with obloquy, with defiance; with charges of intolerance, narrow mindedness, bigotry; and with crucifixion.

That is what happened to Christ. That is what Our Lord said would happen to those who accept His Truth. "If you had been of the world, the world would love its own: but because you are not of the world, but I have chosen you out of the world, therefore the world hateth you. Remember my word that I said to you: The servant is not greater than his master. If they have persecuted me, they will also persecute you: if they have kept my word, they will keep yours also" (Jn 15:19–20).

Hence, I believe that if the grace of God did not give me the fullness of Truth, and I were looking for it, I would begin my search by looking through the world for a Church that did not get along with the evil in the world! If that Church was accused of countless lies, hated because it refused to compromise, ridiculed because it refused to fit the times and not all time, I would suspect that since it was hated by what is evil in the world, it therefore was good and holy; and if it is good and holy, it must be Divine. And I would sit down by its fountains and begin to drink the Waters of everlasting life.

What will faith do for you?

A. It will preserve your freedom. You still live in a world in which you are free to ask questions. Unless you build up some resistance to the organized propaganda that is more and more falling into the hands of pinks and reds, you will become the prey of their law and their authority whose very end is the extinction of your liberty.

Our Blessed Lord said the "truth will make you free". Turning His words around, they mean that if you do not know the Truth, you will be enslaved. If you do not know the truth about addition or subtraction, you will not be free to do your bookkeeping; if you do not know that zebras have stripes, you will not be free to draw them. If you do not know the truth of the nature of man, you will not be free to act as a man.

That is why as men become indifferent to right and wrong, disorder and chaos increase, and the State steps in to organize the chaos by force. Dictatorships arise in such a fashion. Such is the essence of Socialism, the compulsory organization of chaos.

That is why the Church is in full sympathy today with the multitude of people who, stirred by war, at first vaguely and then unyieldingly, believe that, had there been the possibility of censuring and correcting the actions of public authority, the world would not have been dragged into war. Hence, democracy worthy of the name can have no other meaning than to place the citizen increasingly in a position to hold his own personal opinion, to express it, and even to make it prevail for the common good.

B. Faith will answer the principal problems of your life: Why? Whence? Whither? If you are without faith, you are like a man who lost his memory and is locked in a dark room waiting for memory to come back. There are a hundred things you can do: scribble on the wallpaper, cut your initials on the floor, and paint the ceiling. But if you are ever to find out why you are there, and where you are going, you will have to enlarge your world beyond space and time. There is a door out of that room. Your reason can find it. But your reason cannot create the light that floods the room, nor the new world in which you move, which is full of signs on the roadway to the City of Peace and Eternal Beatitude with God.

C. Faith will enlarge your knowledge, for there are many truths beyond the power of reason. You can look at a painting and from it learn something of the technique of the artist, his skill, and his power; but you could look on it from now until the crack of doom and you could never know the inmost thoughts of the artist. If you were to know them, he would have to reveal them to you. In like manner, you can know something of the power and wisdom of God by looking at His universe, but you could never know His thoughts and life unless He told them. His telling of His inner life is what is called Revelation.

Why should we go on saying: "I am the only judge; I am the only standard of truth"? These statements remind one of the tourist who, passing through one of the galleries of Florence, remarked to the guide: "I don't think much of these pictures." To which the guide answered: "These pictures are not here for your judgment; they are your judges." So, too, your rejection of the truths beyond reason are the judge of your humility, your love of truth, and your knowledge.

D. Faith will preserve your quality. Have you not noticed that as a man ceases to believe in God, he also ceases to believe in man? Have you observed that, if you have worked for or with a person of deep faith in Christ, you have always been treated with gentleness, equality, and charity? You could not point to a single person who truly loves God and is mean to his fellowman.

Have you noticed that as men lose faith in God, they become selfish, immoral, and cruel? On a cosmic scale, as religion decreases, tyranny increases; as men lose faith in Divinity, they lose faith in humanity. Where God is outlawed, there man is subjugated.

In vain will the world seek for equality until it has seen men through the eyes of faith. Faith teaches that all men, however poor, or ignorant, or crippled, however maimed, ugly, or degraded they may be, all bear within themselves the image of God, and have been bought by the precious blood of Jesus Christ. As this truth is forgotten, men are valued only because of what they can *do*, not because of what they *are*.

Since men cannot do things equally well, for example, play violins, steer a plane, or teach philosophy, or stoke an engine, they are and must remain forever unequal. From the Christian point of view, all may not have the same rights to do certain jobs, because they lack the capacity, for example, Toscanini has not a right to pitch for the New York Yankees, but all men have the right to a decent, purposeful, and comfortable life in the structure of the community for which God has fitted them, and first and foremost of all, because of what they are: persons made to the image and likeness of God.

The false idea of the superiority of certain races and classes is due to the forgetfulness of the spiritual foundations of equality. We of the Western world have been rightly proud of the fact that we have a civilization superior to others. But we have given the wrong reason for that superiority. We assume that we are superior because we are white. We are not. We are superior because we are Christians. The moment we cease to be Christian, we will revert to the barbarism from which we came.

In like manner, if the black, brown, and yellow races of the world become converted to Christ, they will

produce civilization and culture that will surpass ours if
we forget Him who truly made us great. It is conceiv-
able, if we could project ourselves a thousand years in
the future, and then look back in retrospect over those
one thousand years, that we might see in China the
record of a Christian civilization that would make you
forget Notre Dame and Chartres.

E. Finally, faith will enable you to possess the "Mind
of Christ". "For let this mind be in you, which was also
in Christ Jesus" (Phil 2:5). Though you must meditate
on the earthly life of Our Lord, you should not allow
your mind to dwell exclusively on past events, for by
faith your minds are lifted above the temporal and the
contemporary to the eternal mind of Christ.

Everything in the universe fits into the larger rhythm
of the Divine Pattern, which is denied to mortal eyes.
From now on, you cease trying to find God in creatures,
and begin seeing creatures in God and, therefore, all of
value, and worthy of your love. In the multitudinous
duties of modern life, you will do nothing that you cannot offer to God as a prayer; you will see that personal
sanctity has more influence on society than social action;
your sense of values will change.

You will think less of what you can store away and
more about what you can take with you when you
die. Your rebellious moods will give way to resignation.
Your tendency to discouragement, which was due to

pride, will become an additional reason for throwing yourself like a wounded child into the Father's loving arms. You will cease to be an isolationist and begin to draw strength from the fellowship of the saints, and the Body of Christ.

You will think of God's love, not as an emotional paternalism, but as an unalterable dedication to goodness, to which you submit even when it hurts. You will be at peace, not only when things go your way, but when they go against you, because whatever happens you accept as God's will. You will rebuke within yourself all immoderate desires, all presumptuous expectations, all ignoble self-indulgence, because they bar the way to Him who is your Way, your Truth, and your Life.

With Paul you will say in the strength of a great faith: "I am sure that neither death, nor life, nor angels, nor principalities, nor powers, nor things present, nor things to come, nor might, nor height, nor depth, nor any other creature, shall be able to separate us from the love of God, which is in Christ Jesus our Lord" (Rom 8:38).

CHAPTER THIRTEEN

Hope

It is not so much what happens in life that matters; it is rather how we react to it. You can always tell the character of a person by the size of the things that make him mad. Because modern man lives in a world that has reference to nothing but itself, it follows that when depression, war, and death enter into his two-dimensional world, he tumbles into the most hopeless despair.

A man can work joyfully at a picture puzzle, so long as he believes the puzzle can be put together into a composite whole. But if the puzzle is a hoax, or if it was not made by a rational mind, then one would go mad trying to work it out. It is this absence of purpose in life which has produced the fear and frustration of the modern mind.

To escape from such fear and despair, the modern man usually does one of three things:

a. He sometimes flees from existence by taking his own life. The great numerical increase in suicide, which merits to be called suicidism, is symptomatic of a spiritual disintegration, a sapping of the will to live, a plunge into the irrational and the meaningless self-destruction.

b. He sometimes develops a neurosis due to the disturbance of a godless heart. Neurosis is the common disease of every man who has no hope except in himself. Being "fed up" with life, he becomes cynical, self-centered, asserts himself in loud, boorish, boasting tones to atone for his own inner hunger, nakedness, and ignorance.

Forever trying to lift himself by his own bootstraps, eternally playing the role of his own redeemer, he develops "kinks" and "psychoses" and becomes eccentric because he is out of his center, which is God. The increase of alcoholism is due to a great extent to neurosis and psychosis.

c. While not taking his physical life, he sometimes seeks to kill his psychological life, by losing it in the crowd. Cosmopolitanism, or the flight from the country, is to a great extent due to the quest of anonymity.

The modern man hates to be alone with himself; it makes him think; it reveals the awful cleavage in the depths of his soul. Hence, he seeks noise, excitement, crowds, and the thousand and one other desperate, hectic devices of self-conscious beings to become unconscious. The terror of a crowded tenement, and its hand-to-mouth existence, is preferable to the terror of the inner depths of a soul without God. It is no wonder today we speak of the "common man", the "mass man", and the "man without personality".

There is another way out than suicide, frustration, and anonymity, and that is the way of hope, not natural hope, but supernatural hope that settles your soul in God, and directs your will toward Him. Natural hope, because based exclusively on external circumstances, by its nature is temperamental; it fluctuates, is moody, is high when things go our way, low when things go wrong.

Supernatural hope, on the contrary, is constant and invariable; it believes in the light of the sun even when the sun does not shine because it is based on a sustained collaboration with the Will of God. It may be retorted that such religion is "escapism", and "opium of the people", by creating a disinterest in the problems of this life, through concentration on pie in the sky.

This is not true! Who has done most for the world? He who serves this world only, or he who serves God first and the world through Him? Which man loves a woman more: the one who sees in her a thing of the opposite sex, or the one who loves her virtue more? Who makes the best soldier, the one who loves his life above all, or the one who loves his country more than his life? St. Francis of Assisi never produced any work of art, but who has inspired more art?

The great truth hidden behind these questions is: love of neighbor, the righting of social wrongs, zeal for political justice and equality are all by-products of something higher. The best way to be healthy is not to spend your life trying to be healthy. There is not only sound theology, but profound human psychology in the words: "Seek ye therefore first the Kingdom of God, and his justice, and all these things shall be added unto you" (Mt 6:33). In our modern language, aim at Heaven and you will get earth thrown in!

Just as natural hope makes the will tend toward an object of its desires, for example, it makes the farmer cultivate his crops in hope of harvest, so supernatural hope makes the will strive toward God, and incidentally its own happiness.

How do you react to the vicissitudes of life? Do you rebel because God does not answer your prayers to become rich? Do you deny God because He called away your husband, your wife, your child? In the midst of a war, do you summon God to judgment as the criminal who started it all and ask "Why does He not stop it?"

These considerations may help you to build up a firm hope in God:

1. *Everything that happens has been foreseen and known by God from all eternity, and is either willed by Him, or at least permitted.*

God's knowledge does not grow as ours does, from ignorance to wisdom. The Fall did not catch God napping. God is Science, but He is not a scientist. God knows all, but He learns nothing from experience. He does not look down on you from Heaven as you look down on an ant hill, seeing you going in and out of your house, walking to work, and then telling an angel-secretary to record the unkind word you said to the grocer's delivery boy.

Why is it we always think of God as watching the bad things we do and never the good deeds? God does not keep a record of your deeds. You do your own bookkeeping. Your conscience takes your own dictation. God knows all things merely by looking into Himself, not by reading over your shoulder.

An architect can tell you how many rooms will be in your house and the exact size of each before the house is built because he is the cause of the becoming of that house. God is the cause of the *being* of all things. He knows all before they happen.

As a motion picture reel contains the whole story before it is thrown upon the screen, so God knows all. But before it is acted on the stage of history, God knows all the possible radii that can be drawn from a point in the center to the circumference. He, therefore, knows all the possible directions your human will can take.

Do not think that because God knows all that, therefore He has predetermined you to Heaven and hell independently of your merits and irrespective of your freedom.

Remember that in God there is no future. God knows all, not in the succession of time, but in the "now standing still" of eternity, that is, all at once. His knowledge that you shall act in a particular manner is not the immediate cause of your acting, any more than your knowledge that you are sitting down caused you to sit down, or prevents you from getting up, if you willed to do it.

Our Blessed Mother could have refused the dignity of becoming the Mother of God, as Judas could have resisted the temptation to betray and could have repented. The fact that God knew what each would do did not make them act the way they did. Since you are free, you can act contrary to God's will. If a doctor knows that it is all for your good to undergo an operation, you must not blame him, if you refuse to have the operation and lose your health. Free will either cooperates with or rebels against predestination; it does not "surmount" it.

Because there is no future in God, foreknowing is not forecausing. You may know the stock market very well, and in virtue of your superior wisdom foretell that such and such a stock will sell for fifty points in three months. In three months it does reach fifty points. Did you *cause* it to reach fifty points, or did you foreknow it?

You may be in a tower where you can see advancing a man in the distance who has never been over that terrain before. You know that before he reaches the tower he must cross that ditch, wade that pond, tramp those bushes, and climb that hill. You foresee all the possibilities, but you do not cause him to cross those obstacles. The pilot is free to drive his ship, but he is not free to drive the waves.

While God has given to each of us the power to act, He has left us free to exercise the power. Why then blame God when we abuse our freedom? God will not destroy your freedom. Hell is the eternal guarantee of our freedom to rebel, or of the power to make fools out of ourselves.

The following story illustrates the fallacy of predestination without freedom: In the Colonial days of our country, there was a wife who believed in a peculiar kind of predestination that left no room for human freedom. Her husband, who did not share her eccentricities, one day left for the market. He came back after a few minutes, saying he forgot his gun. She said: "You are either predestined to be shot, or you are not predestined to be shot. If you are predestined to be shot, the gun will do you no good. If you are not predestined to be shot, you will not need it. Therefore, do not take your gun."

But he answered: "Suppose I am predestined to be shot by an Indian on condition I do not have my gun?" That was sound religion. It allowed for human freedom. We are our own creators. To those who ask: "If God knew I would lose my soul, why did He make me?" The answer is: "God did not make you as a lost soul. You made yourself." The universe is moral and, therefore, conditional: "Behold I stand at the door and knock!" God knocks! He breaks down no doors. The latch is on our side, not God's.

2. *God permits evil things for the reason of a greater good related to His Love and the salvation of our souls.*

God does permit evil. In the strong language of Scripture: "He that spared not even his own Son; but delivered Him up for us all" (Rom 8:32). Our Lord told Judas: "This is your hour" (Lk 22:53). Evil does have its hour. All that it can do within that hour is to put out the lights of the world. But God has His day.

The evil of the world is inseparable from human freedom, and hence the cost of destroying the world's evil would be the destruction of human freedom. Certainly none of us want to pay that high a price, particularly since God would never permit evil unless He could draw some good from it.

God can draw good out of evil because, while the power of doing evil is ours, the effects of our evil deeds are outside our control, and, therefore, in the hands of God. You are free to break the law of gravitation, but you have no control over the effects of throwing yourself from the top of the Washington Monument.

The brethren of Joseph were free to toss him into a well, but from that point on Joseph was in God's hands. Rightly did he say to his brethren: "You intended it for evil, but God for good." The executioners were free to nail Our Lord to the Cross, Judas was free to betray, the judges were free to misjudge, but they could not prevent the effect of their evil deed, namely, Crucifixion, being used by God as the means of our redemption.

St. Peter spoke of it as an evil deed, as known and permitted by God. "Jesus of Nazareth, a man approved of God among you, by miracles, and wonders, and signs, which God did by him, in the midst of you, as you also know: The same being delivered up, by the determinate counsel and foreknowledge of God, you by the hands of wicked men have crucified and slain. Whom God hath raised up, having loosed the sorrows of hell, as it was impossible that he should be holden by it" (Acts 2:22–24).

The evil that God permits must not be judged by its immediate effects, but rather by its ultimate effects. When you go to a theater, you do not walk out because you see a good man suffering in the first act. You give the dramatist credit for a plot. Why can not you do that much with God?

The mouse in the piano cannot understand why anyone should disturb his gnawing at the keys by making weird sounds. Much less can our puny minds grasp the plan of God. Martha could not understand why Lazarus should die, particularly because Lazarus was the friend of Our Lord. But Our Lord told her it was in order that God's power might be revealed in the resurrection from the death. The slaughter of the Innocents probably

Pope Francis' Prayer to
Our Lady, Undoer of Knots

Holy Mary, full of God's presence during the days of your life, you accepted with full humility the Father's will, and the devil was never capable to tie you around with his confusion. Once with your son you interceded for our difficulties, and, full of kindness and patience you gave us example of how to untie the knots of our life. And by remaining forever Our Mother, you put in order and make more clear the ties that link us to the Lord.

Holy Mother, Mother of God, and our Mother to you who untie with motherly heart the knots of our life, we pray to you to receive in your hands (the name of person), and to free him/her of the knots and confusion with which our enemy attacks.

Through your grace, your intercession, and your example, deliver us from all evil, Our Lady, and untie the knots that prevent us from being united with God, so that we, free from sin and error, may find Him in all things, may have our hearts placed in Him, and may serve Him always in our brothers and sisters. Amen.

*Our Lady
Undoer of Knots*

saved many boys from growing up into men who on Good Friday would have shouted "crucify".

3. *We must do everything within our power to fulfill God's will as it is made known to us by His Mystical Body, the Commandments and our lawfully constituted superiors, and the duties flowing from our state in life. Everything that is outside our power, we must abandon and surrender to His Holy Will.*

Notice the distinction between *within our power*, and *outside our power*. There is to be no fatalism. Some things are under our control. We are not to be like the man who perilously walked the railing of a ship in a storm at sea saying: "I am a fatalist! I believe that when your time comes, there is nothing you can do about it." There was much more wisdom in the preacher who said: "You run up against a brick wall every now and then during life. If God wants you to go through that wall, it is up to God to make the hole."

We are here concerned with those things outside your power, for example, sickness, accident, bumps on buses, trampled toes in subways, the barbed word of a fellow worker, rain on picnic days, death of Aunt Ellen on your wedding day, colds on vacation, the loss of your purse, and mothballs in your suit.

God could have prevented any of these things. He could have stopped your headache, prevented a bullet from hitting your boy, forestalled cramps during a swim, and killed the germ that laid you low. If He did not, it was for a superior reason. Therefore, say: "God's will be done."

If you tell a citizen of Erin it is a bad day, nine times out of ten he will answer: "It's a good day to save your soul." Maybe there is no such thing in God's eyes as bad weather; perhaps there are only good clothes.

I broadcast to you. There is an engineer in a glass booth who does what is technically called the "mixing". While I talk, he has his fingers on the dial. He controls the tone, the volume, and the register of my voice. He does these things not to make my broadcast poor, but to make it good. God does something of that kind with our actions. We are free to perform them, but He "mixes" them with other actions and other people for the good of the universe and the salvation of souls.

We must not think that God is good because we have a fat bank account. Providence is not the Provident Loan. Sanctity consists in accepting whatever happens to us as God's will, and even thanking Him for it. "Not every one that saith to me, Lord, Lord, shall enter into the kingdom of heaven: but he that doth the will of my Father who is in heaven, he shall enter into the kingdom of heaven" (Mt 7:21).

Do not become impatient with God because He does not answer your prayers immediately. We are always in a hurry; God is not. Perhaps that is one of the reasons why so few Americans like Rome: they heard it was not built in a day. Evil things are generally done quickly. "What thou dost, do quickly."

In a certain sense there is no unanswered prayer. Is there a father in the world who ever refused the request of his son for a gift that would not be good for him, who did not pick him up and give him a sign of love that made him forget the request?

Every moment comes to you pregnant with a Divine Purpose; time being so precious that God deals it out only second by second. Once it leaves your hands and your power to do with it as you please, it plunges into eternity, to remain forever whatever you made it.

Does not the scientist gain more control over nature by humbly sitting down before the facts of nature and being docile to its teachings? In like manner, surrender yourself to God, and all is yours. It is one of the paradoxes of creation that we gain control by submission. You will thus learn to appreciate the advantages of disadvantages.

Your very handicaps will not be reasons for despair, but points of departure for new horizons. When caught within circumstances beyond your control, make them creative of peace by surrender to the Divine Will. From prison St. Paul wrote: "Be mindful of my bands. Grace be with you" (Col 4:18). Others would have said: "I am in prison. God give me grace."

Circumstances must not control you; you must control circumstances. *Do* something to them! Even the irritations of life can be made stepping stones to salvation. An oyster develops a pearl because a grain of sand irritated it. Cease talking about your pains and aches. Thank God for them! An act of thanksgiving when things go against our will, then a thousand acts of thanksgiving when things go according to our will.

"Giving thanks always for all things in the name of Our Lord Jesus Christ, to God and the Father" (Eph 5:20). God does not will the sin of those who hate you, but He does will your humiliation. Things happen against your will but nothing, except sin, happens against God's will. When the messenger came to Job saying that the Sabeans had stolen his livestock and killed his sons, Job did not say: "The Lord gave me wealth; the Sabeans took it away." He did say: "The Lord gave, and the Lord hath taken away: as it hath pleased the Lord so is it done: blessed be the name of the Lord" (Job 1:21).

When anyone asks you "How are you?" remember it is not a question, but a greeting!

If you trust in God and surrender to His will, you are always happy, for "to them that love God, all things work together unto good" (Rom 8:28). "Whatsoever shall befall the just man, it shall not make him sad" (Prov 12:21).

Discouragement is a form of pride; sadness is often caused by our egotism. If you will whatever God wills, you always have exactly what you want. When you want anything else, you are not happy before you get it, and when you do get it, you do not want it. That is why you are "up" today and "down" tomorrow.

You will never be happy if your happiness depends on getting solely what you want. Change the focus. Get a new center. Will what God wills, and your joy no man shall take from you. "So also you now indeed have sorrow; but I will see you again, and your heart shall rejoice; and your joy no man shall take from you. And in that day you shall not ask me anything. Amen, amen I say to you: if you ask the Father any thing in my name, he will give it you. Hitherto you have not asked any thing in my name. Ask, and you shall receive; that your joy may be full" (Jn 16:22–24).

Be not afraid! "For this is the will of God, your sanctification" (1 Thess 4:3). Think not that you could do more good if you were well, or that you could be more kind if you had more money, or that you could exercise more power for good if you had another position! What matters is not what we are, or what we are doing, but whether we are doing God's will!

Place not your trust in God because of your merits! He loves you despite your unworthiness. It is His love that will make you better rather than your betterment that will make Him love you. Often during the day say: "God loves me, and He is on my side, by my side."

Believe firmly that God's action toward you is a masterpiece of partiality and love. Be not like a child who wants to help his father fix the car before he is trained to do it! Give God a chance to love you, to show His will, to train you in His affection. Rejoice! I say again, rejoice: "Thy will be done on earth as it is in Heaven."

CHAPTER FOURTEEN

Charity

America's greatest enemy is not from without, but from within, and that enemy is hate: hatred of races, peoples, classes, and religions. If America ever dies, it will be not through conquest but suicide.

It is heartening to know that there are many attempts to heal these wounds of hate. Principal among them are: pleas for tolerance, for the substitution of new hates, for example, Nazism, for the violent denunciation of groups as bigots. None of these remedies will eradicate hate. Tolerance pleas will not, for why should any creature on God's earth be tolerated? Substitution of other hatreds will not work, for you cannot cure small hates by big hates.

There is more tragedy than we suspect in the fact that we have become most united as a nation at a moment when we have developed a hate against certain foreign countries. Calling other people "bigots" is only a proof of our own bigotry for most generally we ascribe to others our own hidden faults.

Perhaps that is why some politicians call one another "crooked". They proclaim their own innocence by pointing to the mud on the neighbor's escutcheon. Name-calling merely rationalizes our own insincerities, and particularly those names that have never been defined, like "Fascist". Typical of its use is the case of the little girl who, on being asked why she called another little girl a Fascist, answered: "I call anyone I don't like a Fascist." That is perhaps the best definition that has yet been given.

All these remedies are ineffective because they leave our heart unchanged with all its hidden uneasiness. Hate can be eradicated only by creating a new focus and that brings us to the third of the virtues, namely, charity.

By charity we do not mean kindness, philanthropy, generosity, or bigheartedness, but a supernatural gift of God by which we are enabled to love Him above all things for His own sake alone, and, in that love, to love all that He loves. To make it clear, we here set down the three principal characteristics of charity or supernatural love: (1) It is in the will, not in the emotions. (2) It is a habit, not a spasmodic art. (3) It is a love-relationship, not a contract.

First: Supernatural love is in the will, not in the emotions or passions or senses. In human love, feelings have their places, but unless they are subordinated to reason, will, and faith, they degenerate into lust, which wills not the good of the one loved, but the pleasure of the one loving.

Because charity is in the will, you can command it, which you cannot do with natural likes or dislikes. A little boy cannot help disliking spinach, as perhaps you cannot help disliking sauerkraut and as I cannot help disliking chicken. The same is true of your reactions to certain people. You cannot help feeling an emotional reaction against the egotistical, the sophisticated, and the loud, or those who run for first seats or snore in their sleep.

Though you cannot *like* everyone because you have no control over your physiological reactions, you can *love* everyone in the Divine sense, for that kind of love, being in the will, can be commanded or elicited. That is why love of God and neighbor can be commanded: "A new commandment I give unto you: That you love one another, as I have loved you, that you also love one another" (Jn 13:34).

Over and above your dislikes and your emotional reactions to certain people, there can coexist a genuine love of them, for God's sake. Charity is a consequence, not of anything that affects our senses, but of Divine faith. Outwardly, your neighbor may be very unlikable; but inwardly he is one in whom the image of God can be re-created by the kiss of charity.

You can only *like* those who like you, but you can *love* those who dislike you. You can go through life liking those who like you without the love of God, but you cannot love those who hate you without the love of God. Humanism is sufficient for those of our set, or for those who like to go slumming from ivory towers, but it is not enough to make us love those who apparently are not worth loving. To will to be kind when the emotion is unkind, requires a stronger dynamic than "love of humanity".

To love them, we must recall that we who are not worth loving are loved by Love. "For if you love them that love you, what reward shall you have? do not even the publicans this? And if you salute your brethren only, what do you more? do not also the heathens this? Be you therefore perfect, as also your heavenly Father is perfect" (Mt 5:46–48).

Second: Charity is not identical with kind acts. There is a tremendous amount of sentimental romanticism associated with much human kindness. Remember the great glow you got from giving your overcoat to the beggar on the street, for assisting a blind man up the stairs, for escorting an old woman through traffic, and for contributing a ten-dollar bill to relieve an indigent widow. The warmth of self-approval surged through your body, and though you never said it aloud, you did inwardly say: "Gee! I'm swell", or "Well, I've done my good deed for today." These good deeds are not to be reproved but commended.

What we wish to emphasize is that nothing has done so much harm to a healthy friendliness as the belief that we ought to do one good act a day. Why one good act? What about all the other acts? Charity is a habit, not an isolated act. A husband and a wife are out driving. They see a young blonde along the roadside changing a tire. The husband gets out to help her. Would he have done it if the blonde were fifty? He changes the tire, dirties his clothes, cuts his finger, but is all politeness, overflowing sweetness, and exuding charm. When he gets back into his own car, his heart aglow with the good deed, his wife says: "I wish you would talk that nice to me when I ask you to mow the lawn. Yesterday when I asked you to bring in the milk, you said: 'Are you a cripple?'"

See the difference between one act and a habit? Charity is a habit, not a gush, or sentiment; it is a virtue, not an ephemeral thing of moods and impulses; it is a quality of the soul, rather than an isolated good deed.

How do you judge a good piano player? By an occasional right note, or by the *habit* or *virtue* of striking right notes? A habitually evil man every now and then may do a good deed. Gangsters endowed soup kitchens and the movies glorified them. But in Christian eyes, this did not prove they were good.

Occasionally, a habitually good man may fall, but evil is the *exception* in his life; it is the *rule* in the life of the gangster. Whether we know it or not, the actions of our daily life are fixing our character for good or for evil. The things you do, the thoughts you think, the words you say, are turning you into either a saint or a devil, to be placed at either the right or the left side of the Divine Judge.

If love of God and neighbor becomes a habit of our soul, we are developing Heaven within us. The difference then between earth and Heaven will be that of the acorn and the oak. Grace is the *seed* of glory. But if hatred and evil become the habit of our soul, then we are developing hell within us. Hell will be related to our evil life as death is to poison. In Heaven there will be no faith, for then we will see God; in Heaven there will be no hope, for then we will possess God. But in Heaven there will be charity, for "love endureth forever".

Third: Charity is a love-relationship rather than a commercial contract. There are many who think that religion is a kind of business relationship between God and the soul, and that if I give to God, He ought to give something to me; or since I owe Him worship in justice, He owes me prosperity in return.

That is exactly the attitude of the Pharisee who went up to the front of the Temple and told Our Lord that he was an honest man, the husband of one wife, and gave 10 percent of his earnings to the temple. The assumption was that by doing these things He was putting God in His debt, as some moderns do when they say: "I can't understand why God should do this to me. I always said my prayers", or "Well, I have done my bit to religion. I send the church a check every year." In other words: "I do my part, O Lord! Now, you do yours."

If your religion is of this kind, you have no religion. Religion is a relationship, not a contract. Hence it begins not with *doing good*; it begins with a supernatural relation between God and your soul and your neighbor. A right relationship with God, initiated by grace, will inspire you to do good things, but doing good things does not make you a child of God.

Eric Gill once said that "a thief who loves God is a more religious man than an honest man who does not love God." This startling statement has truth in it when understood to mean that the love relationship with God can make the thief honest, but honesty in business does not establish a love relationship with God.

Religion begins with love. "Thou shalt love the Lord thy God with thy whole heart, and with thy whole soul, and with all thy strength, and with all thy mind: and thy neighbor as thyself" (Lk 10:27). The word, "neighbor", here means not the one who lives next door, but your enemy. Conceivably, it could be both simultaneously, as Our Lord implied in the parable of the Good Samaritan.

Translating Charity's commandment into the concrete, it means that you must love your enemy as you love yourself. Does that mean that you must love Hitler as you love yourself, or the thief who stole your tires, or the woman who said you had so many wrinkles that you had to screw on your hat? It means just that. But how can you love that kind of enemy as you love yourself?

Well, how do you love yourself? Do you like the way you look? If you did, you would not try to improve it out of a box. Did you ever want to be anyone else? Why do you lie about your age? Do you dislike your dishpan hands, your pink toothbrush, your athlete's foot? Do you hate yourself when you miss the golf ball? Do you like yourself when you spread gossip, run down your neighbor's reputation, are irritable and moody?

You do not like yourself in these moments. At the same time, you do love yourself, and you know you do! When you come into a room you invariably pick out the softest chair; you buy yourself good clothes, treat yourself to nice presents; when anyone says you are intelligent or beautiful, you always feel that such a person is of very sound judgment. But when people say you are "catty" or selfish, you feel they have not understood your good nature, or maybe they are "Fascists".

Thus, you love yourself, and yet you do not love yourself. What you love about yourself is the person that God made; what you hate about yourself is that God-made person whom you spoiled. You like the sinner, but you hate the sin. That is why when you do wrong, you ask to be given another chance, or you promise to do better, or you find excuses. But you never deny there is hope.

That is just the way Our Lord intended that you should love your enemies: Love them as you love yourself, hating their sin, loving them as sinners; disliking that which blurs the Divine image, liking the Divine image which is beneath the blur; never arrogating to yourself a greater right to God's love than they, since deep in your own heart you know that no one could be less deserving of His love than you. And when you see them receiving the just due of their crimes, you do not gloat over them, but say: "There I go, except for the grace of God."

In this spirit, we are to understand the words of Our Lord: "Love your enemies, do good to them that hate you. Bless them that curse you, and pray for them that calumniate you. And to him that striketh thee on the one cheek, offer also the other. And him that taketh away from thee thy cloak, forbid not to take thy coat also" (Lk 6:27–29). It is Christian to hate the evil of anti-Christians, but not without praying for these enemies that they might be saved, for "God commendeth his charity towards us; because when as yet we were sinners ..." (Rom 5:8).

If, then, you bear a hatred toward anyone, overcome it by doing that person a favor. You can begin to like classical music only by listening to it, and you can make friends out of your enemies only by practicing charity. "If anyone strike you on the right cheek, turn your left"—for that kills hate! hate dies in the germ.

Your knowledge will get out of date; your statistics will be old next month; the theories you learned in college are already antiquated. But love never gets out of date. Love, therefore, all things, and all persons in God.

So long as there are poor, I am poor:
So long as there are prisons, I am a prisoner:
So long as there are sick, I am weak:
So long as there is ignorance, I must learn the
  truth:
So long as there is hate, I must love:
So long as there is hunger, I am famished.

Such is the identification Our Divine Lord would have us make with all whom He made in love and for love. Where we do not find love, we must put it. Then everyone is lovable. There is nothing in all the world more calculated to inspire love for others, than this Vision of Christ in our fellowman: "For I was hungry, and you gave me to eat; I was thirsty, and you gave me to drink; I was a stranger, and you took me in: Naked, and you covered me: sick and you visited me: I was in prison, and you came to me" (Mt 25:35–36).